MW01032555

So... You Want To Date A Younger Woman?

A Guy's Guide To Meeting And Keeping Younger Women

Dawn D Whinetaker

Copyright © 2015 Dawn D Webb

All rights reserved.

ISBN: 151420035X
ISBN-13: 978-1514200353

CONTENTS

·

My name is Dawn. I'm a twenty-three year old woman and I'm writing this book with the intent of helping older men (and I'm guessing if you picked up this book you are an older man) master the art of chasing and winning the heart of a woman fifteen, twenty, even forty years younger than themselves. Age is just a number, right? Of course- but not everyone sees it that way. Some younger women aren't attracted to older men (and to be fair, some older men aren't attracted to younger women). On the other hand, I'm one of those younger women that ARE attracted to older men. I date older men, and I have a pretty good grasp on the good, the bad, and the ugly involved in mature guy/ younger women relationships. Let's start by setting some facts straight. If you're looking to simply have sex with a younger woman, this book isn't for you. There are plenty of sleezy gals of all ages at your local bar. Go there and use your flirting skills to bring them home for a night. If you're looking for a book that will give you true, heartfelt, from-personal-experience advice on having a meaningful and more-than-sex relationship with a woman much younger than yourself, then you've come to the right place.

I'm writing this book from personal experience. Every tip I give here isn't some made-up idea being jotted down on paper by someone who has no idea what they're talking about. Unlike other books in this genre, this book is being written by a young woman who's dated older men, and had very serious, very positive relationships with a select few of them. I've been through this process and I know how it works. I've met men who made mistakes- mistakes I will make examples of in this book. And I've met men who swept me off my feet- with techniques that I will also share in this book.

Before you continue reading you need to know that there is a huge difference between simply dating a younger woman, and playing a younger woman. Many older men don't realize that the things they want in a 'relationship' aren't actually 'relationship things' at all. They fall into an entirely different category. So let's quickly talk about different types of 'older men/ younger women' relationships- and let's make one thing clear. This book is specifically for one thing: guys who are honestly looking for a relationship. The tips in this book are not going to work for men in any other category.

Sugar Babies: The term sugar baby refers to a woman who is in a relationship with a man for his money. And the term sugar daddy, is what the man is called. Essentially this is a relationship where money is everything. Chances are the man is a lot wealthier than the woman and he wants to treat her to the finer things in life. They go on extravagant dates and he showers her with expensive gifts. This relationship, often times, isn't even physical. It's essentially an ego-boost on the man's part because he's in the company of a younger woman. And to the woman, of course, it's a privilege- because she is financially being taken care of in exchange for her companionship. It benefits both sides in the fact that the man receives the attention he wants, and the woman feels cared for and spoiled.

Prostitutes: Indifferent to 'sugar babies', prostitutes are women who are being paid specifically for sex. Often times there aren't gifts or extravagant trips and dates- it's just sex, period. If you're a guy looking for a sexual relationship with a woman much younger than you, prostitutes are awesome- and by all means, go for it if you both are consenting. But when money is involved, emotions aren't. And this isn't a form of 'dating' at all. It's purely business.

Arm-Candy: There are also a few relationships where both the older man and younger woman are in the relationship simply for the appearance of the relationship. The man, obviously, loves showing off the fact he got himself a younger woman (which I find really stupid- because more often times than not it makes him look immature). The woman, loves showing off the fact she's 'mature' enough to get an older guy (again- stupid, because that's an immature reason to be in a relationship). Both people in this relationship are all about the arm-candy. They want to show-off their significant other, but that doesn't necessarily mean there are true feelings involved. It's just a pride-fest.

An ACTUAL Relationship: And then there are real, honest, relationships. In these relationships things happen just like every. single. other. relationship. Things start out casual. They go on ordinary dates. They take turns paying for dates. They exchange small meaningful gifts. Sex happens over time, rather than right away. The 'status' of the relationship doesn't mean anything. Nothing is a secret, but it's not shown-off either. It's just normal. A normal relationship. Just like every other relationship.

So without further ado, now that you have confirmed that you are looking for an actual relationship, and not something else, let's get started.

First and foremost- ask this question to yourself: Why do you want to date a younger woman? Let's go through the common answers- and I'll tell you whether or not your answer is truly worthy of pursuing.

Because you feel young: Okay, let's just start by saying I know very few people who feel old. Everyone feels young. You feel young, because you are young. Age is just a number- remember? But is feeling young really a good enough reason to date a younger woman? Not really. If you're eliminating women around your own age because they're 'too old for you'- you're forgetting the fact that women your age can feel young too. Because remember- AGE IS JUST A NUMBER (no matter your gender). With that being said, if you're open to dating women your own age and younger women, you're on the right track. You want someone who feels young. You don't need someone who actually is young- just someone with youthful energy. Good for you. You can keep reading. But if you're absolutely against dating women your own age, stop right now and go get yourself a reality check.

Because you're physically attracted to younger women: Okay, this is a tough one, because I understand where you're coming from. Most younger women do, physically, look different than older women. With that being said there are still some BEAUTIFUL women over 40 (hello- Jennifer Aniston, I don't look half as good as her in my 20's). But if you're dating on physical appearance alone, you've already docked yourself some points in my book. No matter how good-looking someone is, a great relationship is never founded on physical appearance. If you're attracted to women who are younger- great, but that better not be the only reason you're trying to date younger women. Relationships take way more than physical attraction to be successful.

Because you've dated women your own age and you want a change: Maybe you just got out of yet another unsuccessful relationship with someone your own age, or maybe you seem to make better friends with women your age than you do lovers. So you want a change? You want to try something different? Fair enough- a younger woman could definitely be a change of pace for you. Wanting to branch out and try something new by dating a younger woman is a fair reason, in my opinion, to pursue a woman significantly younger than you.

Because you like the idea of having a young woman on your arm: What an ego boost- right? Toting around some 'hot' younger woman and showing her off at business functions, to your friends, and maybe even to your ex. Wouldn't that just be grand? Maybe for you- but for her, not so much. No woman wants to feel like she's simply arm candy. And if your intentions are more pride-inspired than heartfelt, you're only asking for a heartbroken women and a guilty conscious.

Because you share the same interests as people younger than you: Let's say you love playing Playstation or xBox or WOW. Chances are most women over 40 are not going to share your love of gaming, but many women in their twenties probably would. This can account for a lot of things that simply come with a generational gap. You may be interested in things that women your age aren't- and in that case you may find yourself looking for women who share your common hobbies and interests. If most of these women tend to be younger, then so-be-it. This is a fantastic reason to date younger women, and you've picked up the right book.

Because you have a genuine connection with a younger woman: You may have picked up this book because you've already met a younger woman, and you want advice on starting a relationship with her. In that case, I am SO happy to help. Having an actual connection with someone, no matter their age, is a beautiful thing. Unfortunately age can be a hindrance in many relationships- but it shouldn't have to be. If you're trying to create a meaningful connection, and are a bit out-of-your-element because the woman you're trying to connect with is younger, hopefully I can help. A lot of the beginning of this book focuses on finding younger women to date- but skip ahead a few chapters and jump in on the tips regarding getting to know and dating younger women, if you've already found one you hope to pursue.

"The Daddy Complex"
What It Is, Why It's Bad, How To Know If You Have It

There are a select few older men stricken with what I call 'The Daddy Complex'. What is the daddy complex? There are a lot of different factors that go into this idea, and that's why I separated it from the labels in the previous section. But it's based on the idea that older men often feel like, in a relationship with a younger woman, they need to pick up the 'fatherly' role. This is often done entirely subconsciously, but it's something I wanted to point out early on so the behavior can be corrected and avoided. Basically, rather than taking on the boyfriend role in the relationship, older men will often accidently behave more like a dad instead.

You may fall into the daddy complex category if you have the mindset that you want to care for a younger woman. You want to meet her needs. You want to be the leader in the relationship. That's all fine and dandy (and many women look for that in a man), until you bring in an parenting attitude. Allow me to explain.

You May Give Unwarranted Advice
When dating a woman your own age, you're probably a lot less likely to hand out advice on different life matters. You probably wouldn't go around explaining the importance of a 401K or recommend different real estate options in contrast to an apartment rental. Your intentions are good when you do this to a younger woman; you're trying to help her further herself in life. You're trying to give her the tools she needs to succeed. But often times, all she will get out of the discussions is the idea that you are telling her what to do. You'll also come off eerily similar to another man in her life; her father.

You May Offer Financial Aid
Once again- when dating women your own age, are you likely to offer financial aid? Probably not. Paying for rent, helping with student loans, tossing out extra cash when it isn't necessary may seem like a romantic gesture, but the truth is that it immediately creates an unhealthy dependency on you. I know many women my own age who would willingly accept any extra dollar you hand them, and then-

without even meaning to, get in the habit of relying on you when their bank account is running short. This may sound like an ideal relationship for you- you get the be the knight in shining armor. But it can actually create a very unhealthy environment for love, because rather than wanting to be with you- she may end up staying with you merely because she's dependent on your financial aid.

You May Offer A Sense Of Guardianship

You've seen the cruelties of the world. You've faced the hardships of early adulthood. And if you truly care about the woman you're with- you obviously do not want her to go through the same struggles you may have went through at her age. It's only natural to want to guard her from the 'bad things'. You don't want her walking through the 'bad part of town' by herself at night. You want her to keep her door locked. You want to have a word with her boss about the way he's treating her, or tell her to ditch her toxic friends because they aren't giving her anything but added stress. It's easy to want to guard her, and you can guard her in ways that are sweet. But there's a fine line between sweet, and possessive. And I have noticed that older men do tend to get a bit possessive. Not out of a need for control, but out of a want to prevent the young woman they're dating from struggling. What you need to realize though is that young adults struggle- it's what we do. We don't need you to rescue us, but we do need you to stand beside us.

You May Take The Authoritative Role

By this I mean that you tend to initiate the bigger decisions in the relationship. As things get serious, you may be the one to bring up her living with you (or vice versa), kids, marriage, meeting one another's families and friends. You tend to be in charge of all of the big decisions. As a couple these sorts of things should be discussed between both of you. One person should not be the head of all of these decisions, but I feel like older men especially tend to take on the responsibility of deciding the correct 'times' for things, and moving the relationship along at their pace. Remember that your younger woman is a part of the relationship too- allow her to have a say in things. Simply because you're older, does not mean you necessarily have the right to make all of the decisions.

It's really important to be aware of 'The Daddy Complex', and when you may be falling into these unhealthy habits. Although they may seem insignificant, none of these create a healthy relationship environment, and I do feel they're the biggest things that, as a group, older men can work to avoid when dating a younger woman.

Top Misconceptions Men Have About Dating Younger Women

Before I got too far into this book, I really wanted to take a moment and talk about a few things many older men falsely assume about younger women. There are a lot of reasons that older guys want to date younger girls, but contrary to their assumptions- many of these things do not hold out to be true.

The Sex Will Be Better
Not true, not true at all. We are much less experienced than those lovely ladies twenty to thirty years older than us. We have not yet hit the prime of our sexual prowess. Assuming that the sex will be better with us is often a huge misconception. And I'm talking about myself here- I, a twenty-three-year-old woman, am openly admitting that I suck at sex compared to women ten, twenty, even thirty years my senior. I haven't had as much practice. I don't know how my body works yet. I don't know how your body works yet. I'm still figuring all that out. And yes, that can be fun and exciting. You can teach me knew things. But as enthusiastic as you may be about hopping into bed with someone much less experienced than yourself, allowing us to get in the rhythm of things can be a bit tedious- and honestly, exhausting. You'll need more patience than you would with older women who know what they want and what you want.

We Carry Less Baggage
Older women are more likely to have kids and a history of a family life. They may have a broken marriage under their belt and some

heartache in the past. To a lot of men, older women appear to have more baggage than younger women. Once again, this isn't necessarily true. Younger women have their own baggage. We may not have been married, but we've probably been on our fair share of dates. Many of us may have had some kind of negative experience with men in the past. In the modern age of friends-with-benefits and Tindr hook-ups, many younger women put up a wall against romance to prevent being hurt. Older women have a different way of dating than we do, and younger women- even without the 'extra baggage' can be harder to get to settle, because we do have a higher guard up just simply because that's the way our generation behaves.

We're More Carefree

To a certain extent this is true. We can still go and get buzzed at the local bar every Friday night without much public ridicule. We often don't have kids to care for, and we're in the beginning of our careers where our schedules aren't so tightly wound around a professional life. But that doesn't necessarily mean we're more carefree. Many men have this false sense of hope that dating a younger woman is going to bring youth back into their life. I hate to break it to you- but that's just not always the case. Because times have changed and women now, more than ever, are more career-minded than family-minded, many young women (like myself) are very career focused. We're very serious about our futures, our finances, our independent lives outside of a relationship. Granted, we still want the romance- but we're not as keen on the free-spirit love as you'd imagined we would be. We still have a lot on our plate, and we still have a lot of things we care about outside of a relationship.

We Have More Time 'To Date'

Once again this misconception roots largely back to the fact we're less likely to have kids. Which to many men, means we have way more free time. Granted, women with kids are a bit more tied down to their home life, but that doesn't mean that women without kids aren't equally as tied down to something else. Many women my age are in college, and working a side-job to pay their way through their education. Other women are just starting out in their careers and are working overtime trying to get to where they want to go. Younger women don't necessarily have more time to date, BUT we are more open to making time to date- because it's a societal norm for people our age. So once again, this is partly true. The only thing to realize is that we are busy too, and we do have a schedule outside of our time with you.

Why I Tend To Date Older Guys

As I mentioned in the very beginning of this book, not all women like older guys. But about 50%- half of all women in their twenties, would probably consider the possibility. I'm, obviously, one of those women. So in order to give you a chance to delve into the female psyche of a younger woman who dates older guys, here is why I tend to do so...

We Share The Same Interests: A lot of men my age are into things that don't necessarily appeal to me. Drinking, partying, social scenes, things like that. I'm not really the go-out-to-clubs type. I'm also very politically aware. I enjoy non-traditional activities for my age like attending black-and-white movies, going to museums, and traveling. I find that most men who enjoy these activities are men quite a bit older than me. That's not to say there aren't any men my age who enjoy these activities- just a majority of the ones I know don't.

They're Looking For What I'm Looking For: At this point in my life, I'm fostering children and I have a stable career and I'm not necessarily looking to settle down. Most older men aren't necessarily interested in getting married (they've been there, they've done that). I'm not really interested in marriage right now either. If the right person came along, of course that would change my opinion on that. But as for now, I just enjoy casual dates and very low-key, not super-serious relationships. And that seems to be what most older men want. Someone to be intimate with, and date, but not make a big deal out of.

Things, Just Sort of Happened: I never really intentionally went out searching for older guys. I didn't purposely put myself out there as a young woman available to older men, but more often times than not

I would naturally click with older men, and things happened very organically. Just as all relationships should, my relationships started very spontaneously and in a friendly way. There wasn't anything purposely done about them.

I'm Attracted To Them: Some women, fair and simply, are not attracted to older men. I am one of the women that ARE attracted to older guys on a physical and sexual level. If the attraction wasn't there I don't think I'd put as much effort into getting to know men two to three times my age. But because I am open to physical contact with them, it makes the idea of dating older guys more appealing to me.

Younger Guys Aren't Really Interested In Me: Younger men, I think, are kind of off-put by me. I have a lot of baggage that makes me unappealing to men my own age. I'm a foster mom, so the fact that I "have" kids, does seem to scare a few guys away. I'm also relatively stable in my career- and I am professionally focused (where as a lot of men my age are still in their 'live it up while they can' phase). I don't go out and party or drink. I enjoy things like museums and more cultured activities- that a lot of men my own age have no real appreciation for. Intellectually I feel I click more with older men. With that being said- obviously there are some guys my age who are on the same maturity level as me. I'm not 'strictly dating older men', I just find that they tend to be the people that more often veer to me.

Reasons Why You're Already A Step Ahead Of The Men Her Age

Everyone could use a little pep talk, and I'm going to take a moment and introduce you to the five key points you need to remember. Dating younger women is tough- and trust me, you're going to get denied a few times. That's just a part of the game. But, I promise you, you have a few things going for you that men her age definitely don't.

You're settled in your career.
You know what you want to do. Hell, you're doing it. You've figured

out your career path in life and you've settled into it. Your comfortable in your work position, and chances are- at your age, you've created some kind of name for yourself within your job. Whether you're a beloved member of the company, a boss, an owner, or a successful businessperson in some other sense- you have your career set in stone. Men her age don't. Men her age are still figuring things out. They don't have the stability and smooth sailing that you do. They're kind of up in the air with their plans and ideas. They may have goals, but they're not half as far along in terms of success as you are.

You're financially stable.
Chances are, along with having a steady career, you're also way more financially stable than men her age. I don't mean that you have to be rich, I just mean you know how to manage your finances. You know how to live within your means, and you know how to budget 'the finer things' into your life without breaking your bank. Younger men don't have that privilege or concept quite yet. They don't have money smarts that come with age, but you do. And as shallow as it may seem, financial intelligence is extremely sexy to most women (even if you don't have a triple digit bank account).

You know how to please a woman sexually.
Speaking of sexy, you've had years of practice pleasing women in the bedroom. Even if you spent the last twenty years in a marriage with the same woman- I can guarantee you learned a thing or two about what ladies like in the sheets that men her age don't know about yet. Every older man I've slept with is ten times more aware of my body (and how to make it feel good) than men my age. If you're over 40, you probably know what you're doing way better than any 20-year-old ever will.

You have had committed relationships.
Women love commitment. It's been statistically proven that women are more likely to approach a man with a dog, because it shows that he could commit to something. If you've been committed in the past, if you've put the effort into one (or two- or even three) long-term relationships, you know how to maneuver your way through the rough waters of the dating world. That's really attractive to women of

all ages. We want a guy who's willing to settle down and love us for a while. The fact you've done it before, will lead us to believe that you'll do it again- and we'll adore that about you.

You know women's anatomy.

I mean this in a variety of ways. Obviously you know your way around the bedroom, but if you've been in any long-term relationship you also probably just grasp the basic ways of a woman. You know that we take significantly longer in the shower- so you're not going to complain about it. You know that we have periods, so hopefully you've gotten over your 'grimace stage' when it comes to tampons. You just basically get the concept of women, and we don't need to put as much effort into explaining things to you as we would a younger guy who's still relatively new to the whole 'female' concept. You have no idea how nice it is to be with men who just 'get' women. And older men tend to do that.

SO... YOU WANT TO DATE A YOUNGER WOMAN?

Approaching Younger Women

The Five Different Younger Women You'll Meet As An Older Man

Before we delve too deeply into the idea of approaching and meeting younger women, you need to be aware of the five different kinds of women you are going to run into. Please write these down or mark this page- you'll need to remember these ladies for future reference in this book.

Women Who Are 100% Not Interested
Yea, in brutal honesty, about 50% of all women in their twenties are not going to be interested in older men. That's a fifty percent chance you're going to get turned down (or worse) by a younger woman. I'm telling you this right off the bat, because it's true. And although it sucks, and I don't agree with their judgmental attitudes on dating, it's the way the world works. There are just a lot of girls out there who fair and simply are not attracted to older guys. I'm sorry, but you're never going to get one of these girls to change her mind.

Women Who Are Skeptical, But Not Against Dating Older Men
Standing right next to the girls who are totally against dating older men, are the ones who have never even considered it- but aren't going to totally blow you off if you approach them. These women are the skeptics. They're not the ones you stand the best chance of dating, but they've left the door open for you. If you can hit all of the right moves, you may have a chance with one of these girls.

Women Who Are Interested, But Have Never Dated An Older Guy Before
There are a lot of women in their twenties who are definitely attracted to older guys. I'd say about 25% of all girls in their twenties are more than willing to date someone twenty, thirty, even forty years their senior. Most of these women have never dated an older guy

before- probably because the opportunity has just never come up. You obviously stand a chance with these girls, the hard part is finding them.

Women Who Are Interested, And Have Dated Older Men
Part of the 25% of women in their twenties who are attracted to older guys are women who have, in fact, dated older men before. Obviously these are the easiest women to attract. Most likely you won't even have to go searching for them- they'll come to you. Place yourself in the right situation and one of these girls could do the introduction for you.

Women Who Are Interested Specifically In You- Age Aside
And then, there's the situation where a girl is simply interested in you for you- age aside. Maybe she's not necessarily attracted to older guys, or ever even considered dating one, but she has a connection with you specifically and she's open to acting on those emotions. A select few of you probably picked up this book because you already have a specific woman in mind. Maybe she's already showing interest in you. She fits into this category, and luckily for you- you stand a great chance with her.

How Should You Approach Younger Women?

Probably the most unnerving aspect of meeting women, for men- is just that, meeting them. How do you approach women? When and where do you approach women? And how do you do it when you are significantly older than them, without it coming off uncomfortably? So many questions, so little pages to explain it all in. Let's start with something simple. Where should you meet younger women? And what places should you NOT meet younger women?

Top Ten Places NOT To Meet Younger Women

'Young Scene' Bars/Clubs: There are HUNDREDS of 'older' men who go to bars and dance clubs where primarily younger adults go to party. Younger adults go to these establishments to meet fellow younger adults. And occasionally you may get lucky and find a one-night-stand drunk enough to go home with you (or anyone, for that matter). But you will never find a younger woman searching for a serious relationship here. And you will come off as a desperate creeper 100% of the time you sit oggling at strange women at the bar. Please- I repeat, PLEASE, do not do this! If you're not 23, don't act 23. It's weird, it's inappropriate, and it's setting you and the women you hit on, up for awkward disaster.

Grocery Store: Another place where older men seem to feel it's appropriate to hit on younger women is at a grocery store- and this is just another 'no-no'. I don't care how drop-dead beautiful the girl buying a head of a lettuce is, you don't go up to her. This happens ALL the time- and I can guarantee it's never worked out.

Mall: Okay, here's why the mall is a no-no. There are SO many GIRLS under the age of 18 at a mall. And honestly, many of them may look older than 18. Looks are deceiving. Do not set yourself up for pedophile-of-the-year award by venturing through teen-style stores in the hopes of catching the woman of your dreams. Malls are off-limits for finding younger women, period. We're there to shop, not meet men, anyways.

Sidewalk: I really think sidewalks in general should be banned from the 'places men can hit on women' category. If a woman is walking along, chances are she isn't waiting to be hit on, and she probably isn't open to any ole' person asking her out on a date. There are better times, and better places. If it's dark out, or if she's alone- absolutely don't approach her. There are so many red-flags in that that can easily make any girl feel uncomfortable- a man approaching her alone on a sidewalk is one of those red flags.

Public Transit: Again this is one of those places where women feel very uncomfortable being approached. She's trapped in an enclosed moving area, which also makes it extremely awkward if she isn't interested. Just avoid contact in these areas. It's not the right time or place.

Facebook: Facebook is a great place to meet people who have mutual friends with you- but it's not a dating site. And no 20-something year old woman views it as a dating site. First of all never 'friend' strange women; it's creepy. Message them if you see you have a common interest or whatever, and ASK their permission to friend you. And even then trying to find dates on Facebook is risky business. It's best to avoid it all together, especially if you're significantly older than the girl you're 'friending'. Unless you're actually interested in ONLY being friends- don't send them a FRIEND request.

Craigslist: I mean, this seems relatively common-sense. I've dated off of Craigslist, but all older men I've met on the site have been not-my-type. You're competing with 1,000 creepers when you respond to a Craigslist ad (or post your own ad). Chances are you're going to find a sugar baby or a prostitute responding to you. If you want a real relationship, look elsewhere.

Restaurant: Hands down, if the woman you are asking out on a date is your server- please, please, please do not mistake their politeness and customer-service for them being interested in you. Women can be kind, and genuine, talkative, and laugh at your jokes without having any real interest in you. It's called be graceful and nice. Chances are your server isn't actually in lust with you, and if you do ask her out on a date she may feel like a negative response would discourage a nice tip. Don't put her in that position.

Where They Work: Typically, where someone works would seem like a good place to introduce yourself. With that being said there are a few rules to follow here. If she's a cashier or in a customer-service position where she can't walk away from you- don't corner her with obsessive banter. She's trying to work, and probably isn't interested in flirting. Second of all, if you work WITH her, be sure that you know her well enough before approaching her about a date. Coming off too strong, too quickly, (especially as an older male) will cause a lot of awkward moments in the workplace later on.

In A Position Where You Have Authority: I meet a lot of men who are interested in their younger coworker, and more often times than not- they're that woman's boss. A simple crush is fine- have your crush. That's sweet. On the other hand, do not put that woman in an awkward position by asking her out. If she isn't interested, the fact you're her boss may intimidate her or pressure her into doing something she isn't comfortable with. If you have any authority over the person you're trying to date, look elsewhere. It's not kind to expect a woman to fall for you, when she feels her job or safety is at stake.

Where Should You Meet Younger Women?

Business Conferences: If you guys are working in the same industry- guess what? You already share an interest! Business conferences are perfect places to meet younger women who may be interested in you- simply because they're obviously already interested in what you do. Make a casual approach and ask them questions pertaining to the conference. Be open, be genuine, and don't be pushy.

Museums, Art Shows: I'm not saying every young woman who goes to museums and attends art shows is interested in older men- with that being said, they do tend to have more 'aged' tastes (meaning they're more likely to share interests with guys who are a bit older than them). Casually starting a conversation at one of these places with a younger woman is another totally acceptable, not-creepy, place to approach a younger woman.

Classy, Upscale Bars: Classy, upscale bars are typically a fantastic way to meet cultured young women who are not necessarily going to be off-put by your age. Contrary to the young hip dance club-esque bars, these establishments give off a secure vibe that can allow for nice conversation between strangers. It's an ideal place to meet a younger woman, and most likely- if she's at an upscale bar she realizes there are older men there and is comfortable being approached by them.

Local Dive Bars: Another decent 'bar arena' to approach women in, is the local dive bar. Places where men your age tend to hang out along with the younger crowd. A mixed group. If you're in a place that isn't strictly 'young folks' then you're in a good position to approach a younger woman. If she's at a place where older men hang out, then- as I mentioned before, she's probably comfortable being approached by them (or else she'd be making her way to a place where men her age are more prevalent).

Online Dating Sites: I, personally, think online dating sites are the most successful place to meet younger women. There's a great 'no pressure' environment about online dating. If she's not interested in you, she doesn't have to respond. That simple. Also, you are given the chance to see her profile, and she's given the chance to see yours. You can find common ground without the awkward small talk. The best plus to online dating? Most profiles have a 'preferred age range' option, so you can see if she's actually open to dating men your age. This eliminates all women who are turned off by older guys, lessening your chance of rejection.

Coffee Shops: Read her body language first, but if the woman you're interested in is someone who seems relatively open to contact (and not busy over a pile of paperwork), approach her kindly. Again, just act genuine. Be yourself. In a public, quiet place like a coffee shop- it's generally acceptable to approach someone and talk. She most likely feels safe, and you're not trying to come off as 'hip or young' by being there, so it usually works pretty well for finding a younger woman.

Small Stores, Antique Shops, Book Stores, Etc: First of all, don't go scouring random small shops in order to find your soul mate. Find small shops that mimic your interests. Comic book stores, sports collectable shops, something of that nature. While strolling through the aisles of a store that you're actually interested in, if you happen to pass by someone you're interested in- start a conversation about the items your shopping for. Simple, quick, natural conversation-starters like this one are where about 75% of my relationships have started.

The Library: Libraries are a common meeting place for many people. Women attending college can often be found in a library- and this shows their maturity in the fact that they are career-minded and work driven. Libraries are also full of young women who simply want to read and learn new things. And I know this may sound like a wide range of women (and it is), but I do feel like women who are interested in literature, are a little more open to meeting older men.

Concerts: There's only one reason that I find concerts to be a semi-decent place to pick up younger women and that's because you share a common interest (the musician that's playing). Concerts in general are just kind of a weird place to meet people. The sweaty bodies and loud noise don't necessarily make for the best romantic environment. With that being said, I don't think you'd be out of line to approach a younger woman here, because it is a general meeting place for fans.

Okay, so now you know where to approach women, and where not to approach them- but you still don't know HOW to approach them. There are two ways you're going to meet younger women: online and in person. Each way needs to be handled differently. I'm about to give you some tips- but I also want to point out that you should only do what YOU feel comfortable with. Be confident- not awkward. And if one of these 'techniques' doesn't fit your style, don't follow it. Take the tips as you need them, but don't ruin yourself trying to follow every single 'rule'.

Top Ten Things <u>NOT</u> To Do If You Want To Date A Younger Woman

Before we even get started on what you should do when approaching a younger woman, let's focus on what you SHOULDN'T do. I'm sorry men, but you're pretty dang oblivious when it comes to women- no matter your age. So let's make a few things clear right off the bat- here are ten things you absolutely shouldn't do if you're serious about dating (or even just meeting) a younger woman:

Make Age A Big Deal: SO many men make this mistake. Whether it's out of nervousness or awkward moments or whatever- men seem to constantly make age into a neon sign. They feel the need to tell people they're with someone _____ years old. Or they're constantly making jokes out of it, or pointing it out, or using it as an excuse for differences in interests/sex drive/whatever. But it gets old really fast. If you're older and she's younger- great. You don't need to let the entire world know.

Be Weirdly Cocky: There are some older men out there who think that they are awesome. And it's really stupid. First of all, I don't like guys who are young and cocky. And most mature women don't like guys who are cocky in general. Avoid the vein pictures of you with your shirt off, or you on your yacht, or you in expensive hotels. It's more of a turn-off than you'd actually think. Surprising us with a yacht later on is awesome. Showing it off in the beginning is likely to turn the honest-looking-for-something-nice women away.

Make Your Ex Into A Big Deal: For the love of God, if you had a bad marriage, shut the F up about it. We get it- everyone gets in shady relationships. Some of us get stuck in them for years. And some marriages end terribly. With that being said, when you're constantly ratting on your ex- you come off as the bad guy. If you

28

can't talk nicely, say nothing at all.

Hide The Fact You're A Widower: The few widowers I've dated, were probably the most genuine guys I've been with. For a lot of reasons. I feel like men who lose a wife, tend to 'start again' dating a younger woman- because the younger woman reminds them of their wife at the beginning of THEIR relationship. So it feels right to start at that same place again. There's nothing uncomfortable about it, because they usually aren't doing it for the wrong reasons- they're honestly trying to love again, and hoping that maybe a younger woman can stir up the same romantic feelings they had with their soul mate who passed away. So don't hide the fact your wife passed away. I promise you, it won't scare us away. If anything, it will probably make us appreciate the fact you are open to approaching us honestly.

Be Overtly Sexual: Viagra commercials give off this subconscious message that older men are... less sexually driven. Older men seem to think that they need to make-up for that false image by being even more sexual than normal. They need to give off a continuous sexual essence. And many older men end up coming off very creepy or pushy, because sex becomes the forefront of the conversation. This isn't often done because the guy wants to get laid, it's done because they want to prove that they have a sex drive. Don't worry guys, just because you're a bit older than us doesn't mean we don't think you can perform in the bedroom. So don't overdo it. Be natural, not sexual, with your approach.

Pretend To Be Younger: UGH, this one makes me so mad because Every. Single. older guy I start dating always goes through this phase where they try to be at least a little bit younger than they are. They wear clothes they wouldn't typically wear, or style their hair a certain way, throw around 'lingo' that isn't generationally appropriate for them. Just weird, small, subtle things that make me shake my head. You don't need to pretend to be anything but who you are. If we're dating you, we know you're older- and it doesn't scare us away. So don't put pressure on yourself to act 'young'. Just be yourself, that's the most attractive version of you anyways. And maturity, aged intelligent maturity, is sexy as hell.

Approaching Younger Women Online

How To Set Up An Online Profile That Will Attract Younger Women

USERNAME

There is nothing worse than a poorly chosen username. Ehem, "bigCock69". No... just no. I hope you can sense me shaking my head right now. Do you honestly think women are dying to fall in love with sex obsessed dick man? No, they're not. The best username? Your actual name. "DavidJohnson22" or something similar. It's personable, it's real, it's not stupid. There is no way you can go wrong with using your actual name as a username. Some dating sites don't allow you to use your actual name, in which I case I recommend using one of your favorite hobbies or past times as your username. Something like "HikingGuy56" or "BiggestWhiteSoxFan". Something that says a bit about who you are without being weird or creepy or off-putting. Just, at minimum, avoid something that has to do with your genitalia. That is the quickest way to guarantee women will not respond to you.

ABOUT ME

Generic 'About Me' Section

Every single dating site has an area where you can share whatever the heck you want about yourself. Use this area with caution. Many men have absolutely no idea what to write here and fill in some haphazard definition of who they are (or worse). Don't mention your physique- women don't care if you have a large penis or a six pack of abs. What we do care about is who you are as a person. I see so many men who will casually mention "Well I'm a fit, athletic male" or "I'm a well endowed man". Stop it! Stop it right now- DO NOT do that. That

31

only comes off creepy or self-obsessed. Think of your 'About Me' section as the place where you are introducing yourself to a prospective woman. Imagine approaching her in person on your first date. What sorts of generic discussions would you have? You wouldn't tell her you're fit- would you? No. And online you don't need to- she can tell by your pictures. You also wouldn't tell her the size of your man parts, because that would be totally inappropriate. Don't do it online either. Instead let her know what you do for a living, what you enjoy doing in your past time, your likes and dislikes, and a bit about yourself. Do you consider yourself a logical thinker? Are you more of a spontaneous kind of person? Describe yourself. Let her know in a few sentences the kind of man you are, what you do, what you like doing, and the general things you enjoy and avoid in life. This will be her first chance to grasp who you are as a person, so make it true to yourself. Just be you- and trust me, with 6 billion people in this world, you're going to find someone who loves exactly who you are.

Age and Location

A lot of older men are very timid about putting their age on a dating profile. Honesty is the best policy, right from the beginning. I don't care if you look younger, or feel younger, or are afraid women won't be interested if you're honest; every single woman will lose interest later on if they find out you were lying. So yes, put your actual age. There ARE younger women who are totally willing to chat with guys your age- whether you're 42 or 68, I can promise you there are women out there who will not be off-put by your age. Location is another thing many men question being honest about. I recommend just using the nearest big city. If you live in a big city- then use your actual location. I realize that with online dating you do want a sense of privacy, and a lot of their 'questions and answers' don't necessarily give you that. I do feel that it's entirely okay to change your zip code to a nearby place- or just to the nearest largely populated area. Most younger women do the same.

Interests and Hobbies

This is my favorite section of any dating site, because this is where you give women the chance to find discussion topics (in other words, you're using this area as motivation for them to start a conversation with you- or to keep a conversation going). List out your hobbies and interests and tell them a bit about why you enjoy doing them, or how frequently you do them. If they share one of your hobbies or interests, then you've just boosted their confidence in your possible chemistry. Even if they don't take an in interest in any of your hobbies or interests- they may be curious about them or interested in learning more. This area also gives them a chance to see what you're passionate about- and passion, in any man, is damn sexy.

What You're Looking For

This is another area on most dating site profiles that men royally screw up. Just as in your 'about me' section- don't mention anything physical. It immediately makes you look shallow, and it also can often be misunderstood for the idea that you are purely looking for sex. No woman wants to be a one-night stand, and if they assume that they will be based on a few sentences on your dating profile, you are not going to get a date. So avoid phrases like "I'm looking for an attractive/ fit/ athletic/ blonde (or any other hair color) female". That is one of the most off-putting phrases any man can add to his page. Don't be one of those men. Instead, talk about actual things you look for in a woman. Do you want someone who's more laid back- or are you looking for someone who's adventurous? Are you more attracted to girls who enjoy outdoors activities or fine dining and museums? Use this area to tell the world about the personality traits you're looking for in a partner, not the sexual or physical traits.

PHOTOS

The Ideal "Profile Picture"

Your profile picture, the main picture on your dating site, is one of the most important pieces of your profile. Yes, physical attraction definitely plays a role in whether or not a woman will respond to you. But- in all honesty, physical attraction plays a role in whether or not you're interested in her as well, right? So put your best foot forward in your profile picture. The best profile pictures, I believe, show you from the waist up. This gives the woman an idea of your body shape and a clear image of your face. A face photo is also acceptable. Full body photos, although great, are often very distant- so it's hard to clearly see the person's face in these photos. For that reason, I think full body pictures should be avoided as profile pictures. Opt for the waist and up, or a face photo. Pick something that adequately portrays who you are. Be wearing clothes you typically wear (whether that means a business suit that you use at your job or a nice pair of jeans and a t-shirt). Give the woman an essence of what you're like based on your photo. And I do recommend smiling; it makes you appear way more attractive than some stone-faced man staring into the camera lens.

Add More Pictures!

The more photos, the better. Give women an idea of who you are by letting them see you in a variety of shots. The more pictures you have on your profile, the more personable you appear. You give women the illusion that they already know you, because they've seen many different pictures of you. I know this sounds really ridiculous, but as a woman- I can verify that this part of the female psyche is true. We're way happier to meet up with a man in person who we've seen many pictures of online, than a mysterious man with only one or two photos.

Pictures That Will Attract Women

Want to really grab a woman's attention? Post a few of these pictures on your profile.

You participating in your favorite hobbies: There is nothing sexier than a man with a passion. If you have a photograph of you running a marathon or woodworking or scuba diving- post it. Show that you are excited about something and that you get out and do what you enjoy doing.

You with your pets: Ugh, YES! My all time favorite picture to find on any man's profile (no matter his age) is him and his pet. A lot of women love a guy with a dog. Something about an animal just speaks to our natural mothering, nurturing nature. And seeing a man who shares that fondness of little furry things is very attractive.

You in a clean home: This is a big one guys- but women are meticulous in the details. Watch the background of your photos! If you're standing in your bedroom and there's a pile of dirty laundry in the corner, we're going to question your cleanliness. We pay attention to little things like that. So when you are taking a photo of yourself at home, make sure you're in a clean environment.

You laughing: Tying for my favorite photo with the pets photo is a picture of you laughing. Seeing that you can be caught in a photograph just genuinely having a good time is so unbelievably appealing! If you can laugh that easily, you can probably make us laugh that easily- and we're going to assume that we'll have an awesome time together when we meet in person.

Pictures To Avoid

Just as there are pictures that will steal a woman's heart, there are pictures that will send us running. Here are a few pictures to definitely avoid.

Shirtless photos: I don't know why these ever became a fad online. Do you have a nice body? Great! Surprise us later with it! Leave a little to the imagination. Make us wonder what's under that tight-fitting shirt of yours. Flaunting it makes you look self-obsessed, and desperate for compliments. We won't oblige. There are a thousand other men with slammin' bodies on that dating site- I promise. Yours won't stand out from the crowd. Woo us in a different way instead.

Anything seemingly 'bragging about wealth': There's a difference between posting casual travel photos, and posting blatant images of your wealth. Avoid having a profile full of worldly travel photos, pictures of you on yachts, in nice restaurants and hotels, and driving nice cars. Yes, this will attract women- but it will attract the wrong kind of women. Once again, leave a little mystery to your life. Surprise us with your nice car when you pick us up- it will seem so much sexier then, than it would have in a profile picture.

Photos with other women in them: I don't care if the other woman is only your sister, when we see a photograph of you with another lady our first assumption is that you are a player out to grab the attention of as many women as possible. It's insecure and stupid- I know. We shouldn't be so jealous and quick to judge, but we are. Avoid that jealousy and judgment by not posting photos of you with other women in them.

Photos of you in the past: Many older men falsely advertise themselves with photos of them five, ten, even fifteen years earlier. I feel like this is extremely unfair to the women who are interested in you. When they arrive on your first date, and you don't look quite like you did in your profile pictures- they're going to feel lied to, and that doesn't make anyone feel good. You wouldn't feel good if she was a bikini model in her photos, but when you arrived she was thirty pounds heavier. That was misleading of her. Don't mislead her with younger photos either. Trust me, age does make you sexier in the eyes of many women.

How To Approach A Younger Woman Online

Approaching women online is one of the easiest and safest ways to get to know a younger woman. Specifically, if you are on a dating profile you can check to see the woman's 'interested age range' in who she'd be willing to date. If you fit in that age range- you already have a chance.

Know Your Target And How To Respond To Them

As a refresher, revert back to my original article *"The Five Different Younger Women You'll Meet As An Older Man"* on page 19 to remind yourself of the different kinds of women you're going to meet as an older man in the field of younger women. Once you've refreshed your memory, let's talk about how these women are going to react to you online- and what you need to do in order to get their interest.

Women Who Are 100% Not Interested
First of all, if a women's targeted age range for their prospective partners is nowhere near your age- don't approach them. You're already out of line assuming that you will somehow magically change their mind. They've done you a favor by specifying who they wish to date. Do them a favor, and don't give them the chance to deny you. Unfortunately not all dating websites have an age-range option available for you to view. In this case, you have to go into your approach kind of blindly, and it's likely you'll definitely end up contacting one of these women who just aren't interested. If you get a response similar to "Ew- you're so old, leave me alone." or "What are you thinking? You're way too old for me!!" don't respond. I repeat- DO NOT RESPOND. Leave them alone and let them wallow in their own self-pity, because they've set too strict of dating standards and are eliminating an awesome guy like yourself. You won't change her mind. Don't make it your goal to try to. And don't take it personally. It's her loss, not yours.

Women Who Are Skeptical, But Not Against Dating Older Men

These women are likely to respond in a very seemingly passive way. They're probably going to question your intentions right off the bat- and they'll want to know what you're looking for. If they say something like "Aren't I a little young for you?" or immediately respond to you by pointing out your age (or her own age) in a way that isn't mean, but just genuinely curious- then they're probably 'Skeptic Daters'. By this I mean, they probably assume that you're simply looking for a quick lay. Your goal with these specific girls is to simply earn their trust. Don't respond with some long explanation as to why your age differences shouldn't matter. Instead simply respond with something like, "I just found your profile really interesting and I was hoping to get to know you better, age aside. If that's something you're comfortable with I'd love to talk more." With this, you leave her the option to politely leave the conversation OR to stay. You aren't being pushy, cocky, or too driven. You're simply being polite, and by doing so you've immediately diminished her assumption that you simply want sex. You come off as the nice guy, and with that you have the chance of winning her over.

Women Who Are Interested, But Have Never Dated An Older Guy Before

The response you'll get from these women will typically be very positive. They'll attune right to your conversation and choose not to make age into a big deal. They'll talk for a while, but if they've never dated an older man before- eventually the subject will come up. DON'T be the one to bring it up. Act as if age is not a factor in your interest in her. Leave it out of the conversation. Many men make the mistake of asking "Am I too old for you?" early on in the discussion, and this will put the girl on the hot seat- leaving her wondering the same thing. You never want to make her assume that you may be too old for her; that will push her away. But, if she's never dated an older guy- she'll probably bring the subject up on her own. And when she does bring up your age difference, once again- don't make it into a huge deal. Take a lesson from the 'Skeptic Girls' technique and simply play it off cool. Respond with something like, "Well I feel like we have a good connection, and I really like talking to you- so I don't really see our age difference as a problem." It's simple, it's to the point, it doesn't make age into a bigger issue than it needs to be- and it addresses her issues without making her feel like you're blowing off answering the question.

Women Who Are Interested, And Have Dated Older Men

You'll know these women right away, because they'll respond to your advances with a lot of enthusiasm and genuine interest. They've dated older men before so they're very comfortable with the way things work. Most likely they will never point out your age, and they won't expect you to point out their age. Just be polite and follow my 'message sending' tips within the next chapter to earn your first date.

Women Who Are Interested Specifically In You- Age Aside

Online, these women will approach you- rather than you approaching them. They saw something in your photos or profile that caught their attention and they made the first move. These are by far your easiest targets. Let the conversation flow and follow her lead. These women, specifically, already know what they want and they're going after it. All you have to do is reciprocate.

What Can You Look For In A Dating Profile, That Will Insinuate A Woman Is Interested In Dating An Older Man?

A blatant phrase like "Age doesn't matter to me"

This one is obviously a dead giveaway, but many women will gladly point out that age is not a huge factor for them. If she says anything remotely similar to "age doesn't matter to me" then age doesn't matter to her. Feel free to send her a message.

A self-label like "pansexual" or "omnisexual"

Both 'pansexual' and 'omnisexual' are modern terms individuals use to describe their sexual prowess. Both of these terms are used to define people who are open to dating people of any gender, race, and often times- age. It basically means they do not judge a romance in a stereotypical sense. They're open to unconventional pair-ups, which may mean, they're open to you.

A targeted age range that is at least ten years from her own

You may be much older than ten years her senior, but if she has a 'targeted age range' at least ten years from her age- then it shows that she's pretty open to dating older men. If she's 21, and she has a targeted age range up to 35, then she's willing to date someone significantly older than her. You may not be quite what she's looking for, but chances are she's pretty open minded and if you approach her kindly, she won't count you out of the running just because you're a bit older.

A complete profile, including a thorough 'About Me' section

A complete profile with detailed descriptions and long, thought-out written pieces shows that the woman is serious about finding someone she connects with on the site. The more serious she is about dating, the more open-minded she probably is. If she put a lot of effort into making her dating profile thorough, then she's obviously looking for something meaningful. I have found that women who are more serious about settling down, are also more open to dating older men.

Long term activity on the site

If she's been a part of the site for a prolonged period, then most likely she's had an array of men contact her before- including much older men. If they have not yet deterred her from being active on the site, she's probably open to talking to them. This means, she's probably open to talking to you. Most younger women who only want to talk to younger men will stay on a dating site for a short period while they find a couple young guys they're interested in. But if they're serious about dating, and open to many options (including dating older guys), they're more likely to stay on the site a longer time and meet an array of different people.

Sending The First Message

So you found your ideal girl? You've scoured her profile, admired her photos, and imagined your first date. But- now you need to send that first message. Don't be nervous- this is way less pressure than you are building it up to be. Just keep a few of these tips in mind, and you'll be stealing her heart in not time.

Don't Mention Your Age Immediately: A common 'mistake' that many men make when approaching a younger woman is feeling the need to blurt out how old they are. If the woman's profile said that she is interested in your age range, then don't make your age into a big issue. Approach her with something genuine- and don't make your age (or her age) the biggest focus of your message.

Don't Compliment Her Physical Appearance: Online, SO many men both younger and older use the "tell her she's beautiful" approach. This cliché has been used a hundred times- and I can guarantee that the woman you're approaching is sick of the same old line. Skip out on mentioning her [insert color here] eyes or gorgeous smile. Other men have already told her, and that compliment won't make you stick out of the crowd.

Use Common-Interests As A Conversation Starter: Search women's profiles and find a woman who shares your common interests. Perhaps she's a huge animal lover and you have a dog. Or maybe she's interested in writing a book about dating older men- and you happen to be an older man, who is also a literary agent (*laughs cleverly to myself). Point being, find someone who you can connect to beyond initial photo-attraction. And then let her know that you have common interests. Ask her questions about what she's written in her profile. And tell her a bit about your differences as well.

Accept 'No', And Move On: If, at any time, the woman doesn't seem interested (quits replying, replies with very short 'yes' 'no' responses, or actually says you're not her type) just leave it alone. Do not continue to try and talk to her or rectify yourself. Realize that some women may not be your type- and you may not be some women's type. Don't take it to heart, and move onto the next girl that stands a better chance of stealing your heart.

Avoid The Nudes- Seriously: UGH- men, please listen to me on this one! Let's kick the dick pic fad to the curb, and then run over it with a truck, reverse the truck and run over it again. I can promise you that prior to having a serious relationship no woman in the entire world wants to see a picture of your man parts. Leave them in your pants, where they belong.

Exchanging Messages

Once you've gotten through the first message, and she's responded- it's now you're job to keep the conversation moving without scaring her away.

Do not come off too eager
The biggest mistake I've noticed with older men is that they tend to get a little too eager once a younger woman starts showing interest. They seem to constantly be waiting next to their computer, checking messages consistently, and replying the second she responds. As sweet as your interest may seem, it can easily be mistaken as obsessive or- honestly, creepy. So, as excited as you may be to have a woman you like talking to you, have a life outside of your dating site. Check messages only a couple times a day, and only respond as frequently as she does (if she's only sending you a message once a day- you should only be responding once a day).

Respond with the message length she responds with.
A common rule of thumb when messaging online is that you follow the other person's lead. Respond to her responses with the same length of writing that she wrote. Once again, this shows that you aren't too eager, but you are interested. It also shows that you aren't ridiculously self-centered and you can talk for paragraphs on end about yourself (and as much as she may like you- if she's responding with half as many words, she probably doesn't have the time to sit down and read your eight-page biography). So stay on pace with her. If she responds with only a few sentences, do the same. If her responses are lengthier, write a longer response in return. It's not that hard, just let the girl do the leading, and you do the following.

Don't ask for more pictures unless she does first.
I get it, you want to see more of her pretty face. But, if she has a few pictures on her profile, settle for admiring those ones instead. Many many men will ask a woman for more pictures and here is how girls

interpret that "Do you have any naked pictures I can see?". It comes off shallow when you are so obsessed with their appearance that you want to see more photos, and many women will wrongfully assume that you are asking them to send a snapshot of them with their clothes off. Avoid the miscommunication, or coming off shallow, by simply not asking for more photos. She has some on her profile- that's all you need. (NOTE: If she does not have photos on her profile, it is absolutely reasonable to ask for a photograph or two. But be kind in your approach. Say something like "I've really loved talking to you, and I can't help but be a little curious about what you look like. Are you comfortable sending me a photo? I'll send one in return if you'd like").

Do not 'play games'.
This is a bigger problem for younger guys than it is for older guys, but it's something I wanted to note nonetheless. Many men feel like they need to play some extravagant game in order to win a girl's attention. No- you don't. Games are immature and stupid, and in the end someone's feelings are going to get hurt. Don't ignore her for a couple days to 'get her interest' or talk about other women to see if she gets jealous. It will only make you seem petty and uninterested, and not many women want to waste their time on a man who has no interest in them. Avoid these games at all costs. Trust me, girls don't want them.

Ask questions to continue the conversation.
It's great to respond to her questions and to let her know about yourself- but take an interest in what she is saying as well. Ask her questions related to the topic you're talking about (and throw in a few other questions as well to help start new discussion topics). Showing a sincere interest in what she is saying will make her feel appreciated, and in return- she'll want to get to know you more as well. It's hard to show that you're a good listener online, but you can show that you have a sincere interest in her by asking her questions and giving her the chance to tell you more about herself.

Avoid the topic of sex.
No matter how close you may feel to her or how well you've gotten to know one another online, one of the biggest ways to clear a

woman from your radar is to bring up sex. I know you want to have sex with her. That's totally natural- and that's fine. Just avoid the topic for now. Picture online dating messages as a bar discussion. Would you approach a woman at the bar and tell her you'd like to have sex with her? Probably not. Don't do that online either.

Avoid any topics that may be considered 'not first date appropriate'. Because, online, you can't get a good grasp of who someone is and their tone of voice- avoid really serious topics. Things like religion, past relationships, politics, family issues, and anything 'negative' should just be avoided. Save those deep conversations for in person, when you can talk to one another without the misinterpretation that sometimes comes through typing online.

Get to know her before asking her on a date.
Exchange a few messages with the woman you're trying to get to know before asking her out on a date. Give her a chance to get a feel for who you are- and give yourself a chance to see if this is actually someone you want to pursue. If she seems genuinely interested, after 4 to 5 days of messages being exchanged, feel free to ask if she'd feel comfortable meeting you in real life. If she accepts- congrats. If not, that's okay. You can continue talking to her, but expand your horizons as well. There are some women who just want to talk, and there are some looking for something more serious. Depending on what you want, find a woman that matches your relationship goals.

Plan a date that she'll feel comfortable going on.
When planning for a date online keep it very public. You can offer to pick her up, but leave the option open for her to meet you at the area of the date as well. If she doesn't feel comfortable giving your her home address, or riding alone in a car with you, meeting up in a public place would be best for both of you. Keep the date simple and short. A first date should be simply for getting to know her. In the daytime will probably make her feel most comfortable. And pick a place where you can get to know each other, but won't be alone. An activity like miniature golf, or meeting up for lunch, coffee, or at a nice restaurant are all good first date options in terms of online dating.

Reasons Women May Abruptly Quit Talking To You Online

Some women will disappear after you ask them out on a date, others will just slowly fade away throughout your online conversations. Many men are left wondering what they did wrong, and how they can avoid the same scenario again. There are four common reasons women will leave a conversation, online and never return. Some you can't avoid, others you can.

They weren't serious.

There are a lot of women online, who for one reason or another are not actually serious about meeting someone in person. They may enjoy talking. They may be looking for that emotional connection. They may just be looking for attention and compliments. Or they may be dating someone else- and out of spite, after an argument, are reaching out online to 'cheat'. All of these are very VERY common with many women online. And I'd say about 50% of the time if a woman abruptly stops talking to you, it's because she fits into one of these categories. She got what she wanted from the online relationship, and then walked away. It's not your fault, there's nothing you could have done differently. You humored her for a while, and she wasn't taking it as seriously as you were. Unfortunately, this really can't be avoided.

They just aren't feeling the chemistry.

Other times the chemistry may just not be there. She may not see herself having a serious future with you. Some women will be forward and tell you this prior to cutting off contact, but many women won't. They don't want to hurt your feelings, so they just disappear and stop replying to your messages. This may suck if you felt as though you two were hitting it off, but think about it this way: She saved you the trouble of wasting your time on a woman who wasn't actually interested. Time to move on and find someone who is.

You came on too forward.

A common mistake many men make is coming on too forward. This can be done in a variety of ways. If you reply to messages instantaneously or seem too eager to talk to her- she may think you're trying a bit too hard. If you tell her too quickly into talking to that you 'really like her' or 'love her' (which I suggest avoided- just avoid the L word online), that may make her think you're falling faster than she is. Or if you come on too strong sexually, making comments that refer to a bedroom romp- she may not have the same high sex drive you do, and find that intimidating, resulting in her leaving the conversation entirely.

You did something that turned them off.
Unfortunately, sometimes this just happens. This is why I suggest avoided topics like politics, exes, religion, and anything where the other person may take offense online. Use online dating messages to have light, upbeat conversations- and save the serious stuff for later. One way to get a woman to walk away, is to say something that she takes offense to.

How To Approach A Younger Woman In Person

How To Dress To Be Physically Appealing To Younger Women

Yes, physical appearances matter. They matter to you, and they matter to us. I do think that they're exceptionally more important in older men than they are in younger men. We hold older men to a higher standard. We don't want to 'settle' for someone who looks mediocre, we want someone who looks good. This doesn't necessarily mean you have to have a toned body or emit a perfect allure about you. All it means, is that you need to know how to dress to impress. There are many ways to accomplish that.

Semi-Formal & Formal Wear: Classy bars, museums, and other places where semi-formal or formal attire is accepted are great placea to sport a suit or a tux or just a general idea of classy fashion sense. There is nothing sexier than a man who can show class. You don't need to be wealthy to have poise. Don't be afraid of showing off your upscale side- younger women fall easily for that kind of class in an older man.

Modern and Age Appropriate Clothing: If formal attire just isn't your style, that's totally fine. Wear what's comfortable for you. Modern and age appropriate clothing is best. What do I mean by 'modern and age appropriate' though? Think of timeless items. Dress pants, jeans, button-down shirts, plain one-colored t-shirts, tennis shoes, even gym pants are items that everyone of all ages can wear and look nice in. Avoid silly 'in trends' (for example skinny jeans or graphic tees with modern phrases plastered across the front). Wear what you enjoy, but wear something that doesn't necessarily scream "I was born in the 60's, 70's, etc". Also, don't try too hard to 'dress hip'. Timeless and approachable are much more attractive than modern and awkward.

Ignore The Short-Shorts Men!: Ugh, older boys- I really need to get this through your heads. Short shorts- anything above the knee, is no longer in fashion. It's ridiculously off-putting to see that far up your thigh. There is no quicker turn off than for a man to wear some really skimpy thigh-high shorts, and SO many older men do that! I fully realize that it was in style 'back in the day', but since then it's lost popularity (and for good reason, those hairy thighs are not necessarily the highlight of your body). Opt for shorts that come to right above the knee or longer, and you're good. Anything shorter and you'll send younger women running in a heartbeat- and not in your direction.

Undergarments: I've actually had a lot of men ask me what kind of underwear younger women prefer they wear. It is important. The first time you hop into bed with a woman you want to emit sexuality, not age- in your underwear choice. Most older men I find are really off-put by boxers. I totally understand that, and that's okay. With that being said, if you can sport them, most younger women find them extremely sexy. If not, boxer briefs are your next safe bet. They're what most younger guys wear who want a 'bit of support' down there, and they look good on almost any male body type. At all costs avoid whitey-tighties and any kind of feminine-looking underwear. By this I mean, yes- avoid colors (unless you're wearing boxers where colors are acceptable). Black and navy blue should be your go to choices in boxer briefs. White is okay, although I'd still recommend something darker. Additionally anything that looks somewhat like a bikini just needs to not be worn- it's not sexy. And although many women can overlook underwear choices, there's nothing that can slightly dampen the mood quicker than pulling off our man's pants and seeing that he's wearing almost the same exact underwear we are...

Cologne: I cannot express the importance of cologne. It's just damn sexy. Don't overdo it, a couple spritzes on your chest will go a long way. We just want to catch that manly scent when we lean in a bit too close, or you pass by us. Wear something that will draw in our attention and make us want to get closer again. I don't recommend stereotypical cheap scents, like Axe or Old Spice. Although they're great, they do tend to have a youthful aura about them that just doesn't fit well on most older men. Opt for a classy, personalized scent. Find one that YOU like, in a nice brand, and wear it. Trust me-it will make a difference.

Good Hygiene: This one should be a given, but just to remind all men, being clean is never a bad thing. Wash up, look nice, smell nice. It's really that simple. Greasy hair will never be sexy. Nor will body odor or stained clothes. Be clean, guys. It's not that hard. A quick shower will do the trick.

Hair Cut/ Color: By now you've probably figured out what you like in terms of your haircut. And I will leave hair cut options up to you. Wear what you feel comfortable in. Going to a local experienced, highly reviewed stylist and getting their opinion on a modern look for someone your age could never hurt though. They have a lot of expertise in the area and can help you look attractive in an age appropriate way if you'd like to go that route. If not, I do tend to say that shorter is better for men. There are many women who like long hair, but most younger women who are into older guys would rather be on the arm of a man with short hair. Avoid any crazy styles like mohawks or mullets. Be yourself, and wear what you think looks good on you. But I do think that simple and short is best. Another question I often receive about hair is whether or not men should dye it. Personally, I don't mind gray hair. I find it EXTREMELY sexy. But, in all honesty, not all women my age do. If you've gone almost entirely gray, I would suggest dyeing it. There are dyeing options that allow you to keep some of your gray color while adding in darker tones. I think these work best, but you can opt to dye it completely a darker tone if you'd like. If you've just started going gray (have a few streaks here and there), I don't really think most women would find that an issue, and in that case it's your decision to decide what you're comfortable with.

Facial Hair: Ahh, the inevitable question- to shave or not to shave? Most older men think that women prefer clean cut guys. In fact, it was considered to be a societal norm to shave before a first date. In this modern era, though, times are changing and facial hair is becoming increasingly more popular. Studies have shown that a 5 o'clock shadow (facial hair grown for 4 to 7 days) makes men appear more attractive to women. And I find this to be 100% true in most younger women's preferences of older men. So I think it's safe to say that you can happily grow that scruff out in the hopes of catching a younger woman's attention. It might just get you a second glance.

Know Your Target And How To Respond To Them

Just as with online dating, knowing the women you're likely to run into and how they'll respond (and how you should respond) gives you an edge in dating. Once again, I suggest you head back to page number 19 and reread my piece on the kind of women you're going to meet as an older guy chasing younger ladies. And once you've refreshed your memory- we can talk about how those different women will react to you in real-life (not online) situations, and how you should respond.

Women Who Are 100% Not Interested
If you approach a young woman in a public place who isn't interested in you, she's going to react one of three ways. In the first way, she'll blatantly tell you to leave her alone- or she'll say you're too old for her. At this point, don't rebuttal- just shy away. The second thing she'll do is ignore you. If it seems like a woman didn't hear you, it might just be her polite way of giving you the cold shoulder. Don't continue prodding. The last thing she'll do is be polite, but uninterested. She may reciprocate the conversation, but she'll do so with one-word answers and she'll try to look busy by picking up her phone and texting, reading a book, or putting earphones in. If she isn't responding to you in a way that shows any interest, once again-it's time to cut your losses and walk away. It is hard to grab a younger woman's attention as an older guy, and to be honest you will run into many women who behave this way. Don't take it personally. Don't let it wear away your ego. Just accept that everyone has different tastes and you may not be her taste. Truth is? It's her loss. Don't let it get you down. Move onto the next girl.

Women Who Are Skeptical, But Not Against Dating Older Men

These women are by far the hardest women to pick up in public. They may be a bit interested, but they're also going to come off pretty stand-offish. She'll respond to your conversations and probably be fairly polite throughout the entire time you get to know her- but when it comes time to get her number, she'll back away. Don't push. If she doesn't seem keen on handing over her digits, just back away for a moment. Many men try to persuade the girl to hand over her phone number- and that only makes her feel pressured and uncomfortable. Don't do that. Instead, just say something along the lines of, "I'm sure you get asked for your number by a dozen guys a night. No worries if you don't have any more room in your phonebook for my contact info." and laugh it off. This immediately takes the pressure off of her to give you her number. It lets her know that you won't take offense if she isn't really interested in handing over her digits. On the other hand, your kindness about her skepticism may just persuade her to hand over her phone number after all.

Women Who Are Interested, But Have Never Dated An Older Guy Before

These women will show interest right off the bat. They'll reciprocate the conversation, make eye-contact with you when you're talking, and turn their body into to you to show that they are completely attuned to what you are saying. At some point throughout the night though, they're probably going to throw out a line similar to, "I've never really dated an older guy before." and this is where you need to persuade them that they should date an older guy. Unlike online, where I tell you to simply dismiss their claims- in person the woman honestly does need persuasion to give you her number. She needs to be persuaded that she wants to date an older guy. The best response I can offer you to give in a situation like that is to turn the question around on her. In other words- ask her what SHE thinks of dating an older guy. Say something like, "Well has our conversation opened you up to the possibility?". If she's been enthusiastically talking to you for a while, then she's going to answer, "Yes." and at this point- you've just been given the invitation to ask for her number.

Women Who Are Interested, And Have Dated Older Men

Just as with the women I was just speaking about, these women are going to give you their full attention. They are going to show a clear interest in what you are saying, and probably have a lot of comfortable flirtatious body movement around you (brushing your arm, leaning in closely to hear what you are saying, etc). With that being said, at no point will they probably point out your age. And when you ask them for their number, they'll probably willfully hand it over- because you're exactly the kind of person they're interested in dating.

Women Who Are Interested Specifically In You- Age Aside
Online, these women will approach you first. In person- these women will either approach you first or give you a clear incentive to approach them. They may wink at you, smile, wave you over, or even initiate some small talk. At this point, she's given you a clear signal that she's ready for you to make the next move and keep the conversation going. If she was the one to start the contact, feel free to ask for her number any time after the conversation begins to hit a high point. Most likely, she'd been waiting for you to do so from the moment you began talking.

The Perfect Way To Pick Up A Younger Woman In Person

Being denied in person by women just seems to be the norm. You expect a 'no' and are pleasantly surprised when you finally find a woman who actually seems interested in talking to you. I'm not saying your game is wrong, but it may not be as strong as it could be. You need to stand out from the crowd. Don't be just another guy offering her your attention.

Smell nice, dress nice, be nice

Your first impression honestly is made on your appearance. You don't have to be drop dead handsome to appear nice. Practice good hygiene, be clean, wear decent clothes that fit well, put on some cologne (just not too much cologne). It will go a long way in how girls perceive you. If you look nice and put together, they're going to be a lot more open to talking with you than they would if you looked like you've been living on the streets.

Watch for 'welcome signs'

If a woman finds you attractive from across the room, she will give you 'welcome signs', and by this I mean she will give off subtle cues that she is interested in talking to you. If you make eye contact with a woman more than three times in a short time span, then you're in her line of sight, and most likely she's looking at you as often as you're looking at her. That's a good thing! Additionally, if she smiles- it's her way of showing you that she's not a 'big scary woman who's going to be rude when you approach her'. A smile makes her approachable, and open to being approached. If you are already sitting next to her, if she points her body towards you (crossing her legs in your direction, subtly turning her chair towards you, leaning her head slightly to face your direction, looking in your general direction), then these are signs that she's probably open to speaking with you, but maybe too shy to make the first move. Just look for a few small signs that she may be approachable. Not all women want to be hounded on at a bar, so look for the women who have an open and happy body language about them. Also, if women respond kindly to other older men who approach them- they're good targets as well.

Just a simple "Hey" can go a long way

Ignore the pick-up lines. They come off as forced and trust me- if she's pretty enough she's heard every single one, before. So opt for a simple "Hey" instead and then feed off of her body language. If she tosses you a quick 'hey' and then goes back to focusing on her friends, or phone, or whatever she's doing, she probably isn't interested. On the other hand if she smiles, makes eye contact, responds and then waits for you to continue the conversation- you're in. You can walk away if the "Hey" doesn't go as well as you thought it would without being denied, and if it does go well- you have an open invitation to keep talking.

Talk before you offer her a drink

If you're at a bar, keep in mind that you are competing with many other men who have likely approached the same girl you are approaching. Many girls at bars are used to being picked up by being offered a drink. Stand out from the crowd by not taking that tactic. Talk first, get to know her without buying her a drink. Let her know you're interested in her- not getting her drunk. If you want to buy her a drink later, feel free. But it doesn't need to be the first part of your greeting (or honestly, any part of your approach- sometimes not buying her a drink can make you stand out even more).

Keep the conversation upbeat and focused on her

Avoid bragging, complaining, cursing, and talking about your ex (or any other relationship for that matter). Keep the conversation friendly and hooked to a positive topic. And even more than that- keep the conversation focused on her. Don't drill her with an interview, but ask questions pertaining to what she's talking about. Motivate her to continue talking to and spending time with you.

Leave, with the invitation for her to find you again

Many men will overstay their welcome. Keep your first conversation at about 5 minutes in length and then make an excuse as to why you need to leave (ie, your buddies are waiting for you, you're going to get a drink, etc). Let her know you'd like to see her again and if she's around, she should stop and chat. This gives her a way to find you, which will give you a chance to test and see if she's actually interested, without getting denied.

What should you do if she doesn't come looking for you?

Many women won't take the initiative to approach you, but that doesn't necessarily mean that they're not interested. Often times women just aren't used to being the ones that approach the guy. An easy way to approach the same woman later on, is to simply 'accidently' run into her again. Teasingly say something like "I see you got too busy to say 'hi'" and smile. Let her know you're teasing, not being pushy. If she reciprocates with an apology or an excuse for not finding you, or even a laugh- she's probably interested. If she simply says something along the lines of "Ya..." or a mere "I got busy" she probably had no intentions of finding you. Also pay attention to her body language. If she turns towards you, makes eye contact, awaits you to further the conversation- you're in. At this point, ask her for her number with a genuine line like "I had fun talking to you earlier, but we both are obviously pretty busy at the moment. Can I get your number so I can get to know you better some other time?" It's classy. It doesn't seemed forced. It's not sleezy. It's genuine. And I can guarantee it will work better than any other absurd dating tip you hear from other 'pick up experts'.

How To Text/ Call A Girl Once You've Gotten Her Number

Probably the biggest difference in most older men's generation and younger woman's generation, is the way people communicate following an initial introduction. It used to be very common for the man to call within a day or two of the first meeting. Now, times have definitely changed. With cell phones not only can you call within just an hour of meeting someone- you can text as well. It raises an array of questions and puts a lot of pressure on a lot of older men who are used to a more 'traditional' approach to dating.

How do you text or call a woman once you've gotten her number? The most common question I receive is, "How long should I wait before I text or call her? And should I text or call?" Personally, I feel that the following day is best. Sometime in the afternoon or early evening when she's not likely to be busy. If you met her Friday night, get a hold of her later in the day on Saturday. There's no real mathematical approach to the 'right time' to text or call a woman. I don't like that many 'pick up artists' teach men to wait longer than 24 hours "to grab the woman's attention". I feel that those games are pointless, and if the woman's interested in you she's not going to care if you waited longer than a day to get a hold of her. The only time I think it's 'too soon' to call or text is within the same evening you got their number. Most likely you've picked up their digits at a social event and she's having a night out. She's busy. It's definitely not the right time to get a hold of her. Wait until a reasonable time of the day, the following day, and try her then. Now- to answer the other question; should you text or call? This is a tough one. Many younger women expect older men to call, because it's what is more widely accepted in your generation's dating standards. With that being said, in the era of texting, I don't think many women would be off-put by a text. Do what you're comfortable with. Texting can often take the pressure off, because if she decides she wasn't actually interested she doesn't have to answer. It also gives you more of an edge, because you don't have to battle awkward silences or nervous first-time phone conversations.

I believe the best way to text someone after an initial first meeting is to re-introduce yourself and then ask a question. This simply reminds them who you are, and also gives them a reason to respond. Say something like, "Hey this is John from [insert place you met]. It was nice to meet you yesterday. Did you enjoy the rest of your night?" Simple, easy, approachable. The best text. Nothing too over the top. Nothing stupidly witty. It doesn't look like you're trying too hard. And it gives them a way to keep the conversation going, because you asked a question.

If she doesn't text back, I truly believe that you shouldn't text again. There is a one in a million chance that the text didn't go through- so you don't need to text and ask her if she got your text. Most likely she did, and if she didn't- call it fate's way of pointing you in a different direction. Continuing to text, even though she hasn't responded, just gives off a vibe that you're a bit too eager, and she'll lose interest very quickly after that. Everyone woman wants to feel adored, no woman wants to feel stalked. There's a fine line between texting and being borderline-creepy. Don't text back until she's replied first. And if she doesn't reply, I'm sorry- but it's probably her kind passive aggressive way of telling you she's not interested.

If she does text back it's important to be patient in your response. Phones make communication so convenient. It's easy to text back and forth constantly for hours on end. But it's important to have a life away from your phone. Make a point to only chat once or twice a day. Imagine text messages the same way you'd use phone calls. You wouldn't spend all day with your phone glued to your ear talking to them. Don't spend all day exchanging haphazard small chat in texts.

Sit down for a night time chat each evening or exchange a few words in the morning. Keep it simple. Treat texts like phone calls, and only make an effort to sit down and talk when you both have the time and energy to put effort into your discussions.

Dating A Younger Woman

Top Things NOT To Do On Your First Date With A Younger Woman

So you finally arranged a first date? Congrats! Before I even delve into the ins and outs of your first date experience, let me strictly tell you what not to do. Avoid these if at all possible when seeing a younger woman for the first time.

Call Your Ex Wife Your 'Ex Wife': Okay, just stop for a second. If you're dating a woman in her twenties, and you've been married before- chances are she hasn't been married before. So don't refer to your 'ex' as your 'ex wife'. Call her your 'ex'. That's it. Most likely she has 'exes' as well. She can find common-ground with you on that. But if you're constantly blabbing on about a ruined marriage, you're going to scare her off, because she cannot relate to that.

Bring Up Your Kids: Eesh, I know this is a tough one- especially if you're a proud father. Don't keep your kids a secret. Casually mention them. But don't pull out pictures and list all of their accomplishments UNLESS she initiates that conversation. Keep it low-key for the first few dates. She should be focused on getting to know you- not your family. The seriousness of kid-introductions can turn a younger woman away very quickly, because it's not often something they've dealt with before or feel prepared to handle early in a relationship.

List Off A Hundred Past Accomplishments: We realize you're older than us, and you've had more experiences in life. Chances are you've traveled places we haven't, you're farther along in your career, and you're just genuinely more successful. But you don't need to brag. Let those things flow out on their own, in natural conversation.

Boasting is a turn-off, no matter your age. Older men just seem to think it's attractive that they've accomplished so much- and it IS. But it isn't attractive to brag about yourself constantly.

Make Your Age Into A Joke Or A Discussion: If a younger woman accepted a date with you, she most likely did so because your age wasn't a factor. So don't make it a factor. And this is a mistake SO many older men make. They think they're lessoning the tension by picking fun at how 'old' they are. In all reality, it just accentuates the creepy-ness of everything. Age shouldn't be an issue, so please don't make it the focus of the date.

Pick Fun At Her Age: The same goes for her age. If she's younger than your daughter (or so young she could be your daughter) don't point that out. It's weird. And correlating us with your child is not going to make you sexually appealing. Stick to basic date-topics and leave the age difference at the way side.

Ways To Make A First Date Less Awkward

First dates, no matter the situation that lead up to them, are inevitably awkward and uncomfortable. Take a second, breathe, and calm down. It's going to be okay- in fact, it's going to be awesome. And there are a few simple steps you can take to make sure it's even better than the last ten first dates you've had.

Meet in a mutual, not busy area

Offering to meet in a place where you're in public, takes away the fear many women have for their own safety. With our nation becoming more and more 'rape aware', women are reasonably skeptical of meeting up with men in a private place for the first time. So opt for somewhere public, BUT QUIET! This is the important thing. First dates are awkward enough without a mess of voices competing with your conversation. Avoid loud bars, or honestly- anywhere with alcohol. Alcohol just doesn't make for a good first impression. Go somewhere nice, in the daytime, where you can make the date short and stress-free. A coffee shop, smoothie place, small cafe- anywhere where you can easily hear one another and have a quick, genuine meeting that you'll both enjoy.

Sit next to them, not across

When you sit directly across from someone you are making eye contact with them the entire time. They are the sole focus of your visual area. This can make awkward silences even more difficult, because you can't casually look away. Sitting side by side with someone (or catty-corner at a table) allows you to make eye contact with them, but also naturally break it at times when there's a lull in the conversation.

Initiate touch at the beginning of the date

If you want a kiss later in the date, initiate touch from the very beginning. A friendly hug or pat on the shoulder can break the ice when it comes to touching. Don't be ridiculously 'groping feeling', but natural casual touch should be a part of your conversation. Keep it light, not creepy- and you'll both feel more comfortable leaning in to lock lips later in the night.

Engage in the conversation

One of the worst date situations is when someone is merely replying with one word responses to your questions. "Yes" "Mmhmm" "Oh nice" "No" are some of the hardest things to continue a conversation from. Do not- I repeat DO NOT be that person. Engage in the conversation. Talk about things you know, about things you're passionate about. Ask them questions about themselves. Don't be afraid to talk a bit, you won't come off annoying- we promise. You'll come off involved in the conversation.

Don't let awkward silences be awkward

If you start to over think awkward situations, it will only make them more awkward. Don't let a lull in the conversation ruin your confidence. Every single first meeting of someone is going to have some kind of quiet moment. It's nothing to fret about. Look around, think of a topic, let it pass. It's no big deal. Don't let awkward silences be awkward.

Things Younger Women Expect Older Men To Do That They Don't Expect Men Their Age To Do

As unfair as it may be for younger women to have higher standards for older men- we do. We definitely expect more out of you, because with age should come maturity. Most older men I've met do these things naturally, but they are things I want to point out nonetheless- so you are aware of them. Without further ado here are things younger women expect older men to do, that they don't expect younger guys to do.

Be gentleman/ have common courtesy
You come from an era where being a gentleman was more widely applauded. They expected you to hold doors, pull out chairs, offer your jacket, have good table manners, be polite, and ask permission before kissing her. The same thing -should- be expected of younger men, but honestly often isn't. With that being said, our generational gap has lead us to believe that you should know how to treat a

woman like a lady; and you should.

To call instead of text

Many younger women prefer texting over a phone call, but when we date a man older than us, we associate his dating style with different generational standards. One of those standards is for you to make a phone call rather than a text, as the relationship blossoms and we begin talking regularly. I'm not sure why many young women (including myself) take offense when an older man chooses to text instead of call, but the act of picking up the phone, especially with older men, is very appreciated.

Not to pressure sex

Younger men have a higher sex drive than older men. That's a scientific fact. And with that knowledge, women often assume that older men will not pressure sex in the same manner younger men do. Younger men will often be the first ones to initiate or bring up sex- and they'll do so relatively quickly. We often think that older guys will wait, and let us show interest in going into the bedroom before they make a move. This is one reason many younger women would much rather date an older man; the no-sex-pressure attitude makes dating significantly less stressful on many women.

Be willing to please her before yourself

Along with the assumption that the pressure to have sex will not exist, younger women also often believe that older men are more willing to please them. In fact, my experience has been that older men WANT to please me, not just themselves. That is such a huge turn on and it is one of the main reasons that I've grown to prefer dating older guys.

Going To The Bedroom: Sealing The Age Gap Between The Sheets

How Soon Should You Have Sex With A Younger Woman?

This is a common question I receive from many older men. How soon should you expect to sleep with the younger woman that you're dating? The truth is, I cannot give a definitive answer on that. Each woman is different. Each situation is different. There is not necessarily a key time frame in which you are guaranteed to have sex. I think it's a good rule of thumb to not go into the first date expecting sex, but not eliminating the chances of it. If you've both hit it off really well and she seems to genuinely be showing interest- reciprocating physical touch and staying attuned to your conversation, sex shouldn't be out of the question. With that being said, most successful relationships move slower than that.

Some women have different comfort levels than other women. Some women may be waiting until marriage. I think most modern young women, on average, will sleep within a men between the first two weeks and three months of dating. After the fourth week, if sex hasn't been brought up- I do think it's an entirely appropriate topic to discuss it (granted you've been on at least one date a week for those four weeks- and she is showing interest in you).

Younger women definitely expect older men to be more patient with them sexually. If an older man gets pushy or is too forward about sex too soon, it will often scare younger women away. There are many "pick-up artists" (and I use that term loosely) who will swear they have the techniques for older guys to easily get younger women in bed. I call BS on their techniques, because as a younger woman- I know younger women's expectations. And we definitely expect older men to be a lot less pushy when it comes to sex than we do younger men. So whatever 'techniques' or 'tips' those "pick-up artists" have given you. Throw them out the window. They may work on a select few women- but being courteous and not playing stupid little mind games will work significantly better on many more women.

A woman will clearly give you signs when she's interested in having sex with you. But, as you probably know, women are subtle in their approach- so it's your job to pick up on those signs.

How Do You Know If A Younger Woman Is Ready To Sleep With You?

Like I previously mentioned, most younger women expect older guys to move slower in the bedroom, but when they really start to like you- they're naturally going to try to initiate sex (unless they plan to wait due to religious beliefs or personal values- in which case, I'd hope by the fourth week you would have discussed that and been comfortable with her decision). So, from date one, to date one hundred- here are the ways a woman is going to let you know that she is, in fact, interested in getting physical with you. Women won't usually just give off one of these signals- they'll give off many.

Sitting very close to you
If a woman is not interested in having sex with you, she isn't going to sit very close to you. But if she's sitting right next to you- with her leg brushing yours, or your her foot next to yours, her hand holding yours, or her side pressed against yours- then she's showing you that she's open to even more touch. Women are very attuned to physical moments. They never 'accidently' sit too close to someone. So if she's sitting very close to you, it's entirely intentional, and she's showing you that she's open to more intimate touching.

Leaning in to hear what you're saying, even in a quiet environment
Many people unintentionally lean close to someone during a discussion if they're physically attracted to them. They want to hear what they're saying, but they also want to be physically closer to them to show that they're truly involved in the conversation. Not only is she taking the initiative to show that she is entirely focused on what you're saying, she's also showing you that she physically doesn't mind getting closer to you.

64

Reciprocating touch

If you brush her arm, rub her thigh, or hold her hand without her pulling away- it shows that she's comfortable with you. If she returns the favor, she's showing that she is open to more touching. It's perfectly fine to be a little touchy-feely, but don't overdo it. A quick shoulder massage or holding hands across the dinner table can be romantic and genuine. If she doesn't push you away from that touch, that's a good sign. But if she touches you in return- it's an even better sign. With this being said, I would like to point out that on a first date these 'touching moments' are not appropriate unless she initiates them first. It can quickly make many women feel uncomfortable if you're touching them sensually on the first date. Save that for once you've gotten to know one another a little better (unless she starts touching you first).

Initiating touch

Which brings me to my next point- if SHE initiates the touching, even though you haven't put in effort into touching her first, then she's making the first move in letting you know that it's okay to touch her. At this point it's totally fine to reciprocate touch, and to assume that more intimate touching may be in store later in the night.

Kissing passionately

There's a difference between a sweet, quick 'goodbye' kiss, and a lingering make-out session. You can often tell how far a woman is willing to go, by the tenacity in which she kisses you. If I'm not keen on sleeping with a guy I will offer him a kiss on the cheek, a quick peck on the lips, or possibly a minute-long French kiss without a lot of heat exchanged. On the other hand, if I'd like to invite the guy into my bedroom (or have him invite me back to his place), I will let the kiss get more passionate. At this pace I'll kiss him for longer periods of time, I may put my hands in his hair or the back of his neck- or around his waist, I may press my body into his and kiss him with more pressure. I mean, if she's kissing you for sex- you'll know. There's a difference between the way she kisses you when she's ready to go home for the night, and the way she kisses you when she wants to keep the night going. Compare her current kiss to her past one, and wait for the time when she seems eager and enthusiastic about the make-out session. That's the ideal time to take things a step further.

Wearing provocative clothing

Women are fully aware of the fact that men are visual creatures, and if we go out of our way to show a bit of extra skin a few dates in- we're giving you the signal that it's probably okay to slip that dress off at the end of the night. We're very good at using subtle indicators to get what we want. Wearing provocative clothing that shows more skin than we typically do is one of our favorite ways to grab your attention.

Being loose with her alcohol consumption

Many women, when anticipating sex, will begin to drink more in an attempt to alleviate their nerves. An increase in alcohol consumption can also be a sign that she is not enjoying herself and is reaching for intoxication in the hopes of bettering the night. Pay attention to her other actions as well. If she's showing interest in other ways, along with reaching out for more alcohol, she's probably ready for sex. Unfortunately, when she begins to get intoxicated, you've lost your chances at sex. There's a fine line between letting her drink to cure her nerves, and letting her get drunk. If you have genuine interest in having sex with her- do not let her get drunk. If you're paying, you should be in charge of how many drinks she orders. And if she's reaching a limit that you think is too high, cut her off by closing the tab. It's important to remember than an intoxicated person can NOT give consent, and having sex with them IS rape. So although she may actually be interested, if she's a bit too tipsy- keep your hands to yourself for the night. She'll appreciate you for it the next morning, I promise- and you'll be rewarded with much more satisfying sober sex later.

Mentioning sex, being open to discussing it

At some point in every relationship the discussion of sex will come up. As I've mentioned before, by the fourth week (if you've been on at least one date a week), I do feel it's appropriate to bring up sex and to discuss her comfort level. But, some women will bring up sex on their own before this time. If she's bringing up the topic of sex by herself and she's open to the idea- she's telling you in no uncertain terms that she's comfortable with the idea and you can definitely make the first move. Additionally, if she is open to discussing sex with you and shares her interest in having sex once you've brought up the topic- again, she's given you the go ahead to initiate sex.

Accepting your invitation for an activity at your home

By the fourth to fifth date in, I do feel it's entirely acceptable to invite a woman for a date back at your place. Offer something that fits into your previous dating style. It can be something eloquent like a romantic home cooked dinner, or even something simple like a movie night- she gets to pick the flick. Dates held in the privacy of your own home hold the notion that sex will follow later in the night. If she accepts a date that is taking place in the privacy of your own place, then she's acknowledging the fact that you have intentions of taking things further and she's agreeing that she's comfortable with that. As in any situation- I would never say that you should expect sex simply because she accepts an invitation to a private date. But I do feel that generally it's a very positive sign that she's willing to take things further. On the other hand, if she excuses herself home early in the night- she probably wasn't interested in sex. If she hangs around later into the evening, I would almost guarantee that she's waiting for you to make a move.

Inviting you back to her place

Lastly, the most obvious way a woman will initiate sex with you (without coming out and blatantly requesting it), is to invite you back to her place- especially in the evening following a date. This is a pretty typical way for couples to take things a step further. I would argue that it's become a societal norm. So if she's offering for you to come in as you're dropping her off, you can safely assume that she has more in mind than just sharing a glass of wine.

Bringing Up Sex

So I've mentioned quite a few times now, that by the fourth week into seeing a woman I feel it's fair to bring up sex. What I haven't told you is HOW to bring up sex. It's kind of an odd topic to get started on if she hasn't shown any interest in discussing it. The truth is, it's not something you bring up over dinner- it needs to be done in a private place when you're both already being physical. I always tell men, that if they are a bit shy to bring up sex- wait until they want sex (aka- amidst a make-out session). In the heat of the moment, you can literally say something like, "Would you be comfortable if we took this further?" and it will be an appropriate thing to say. There are two replies. Either she can say "Yes" and wah-lah, you guys are having sex. Or she can say, "No." at which point, don't push her- but I do think it's absolutely fair that you can ask why. With that being said, I think just blatantly saying "Why?" is a bit rude, and pushy. Instead opt for something like, "I'm totally okay that- but just out of curiosity, can you explain why? I feel like we have a lot of physical chemistry, and I won't push you if you're not comfortable, but I'd like to know what I can do to make you more comfortable." With this phrase you've accomplished three things.

1) You've let her know that you are not going to push her to have sex. You respect her decision and you won't go beyond her boundaries.

2) You've given her the option to explain herself, and for you to figure out what you can do to help her feel more comfortable with the idea of moving to the bedroom.

3) You've let her know you were interested in having sex, by letting her know you want to make her comfortable enough to do so.

Listen to what she says and respond with compassion and understanding. Women have an array of reasons for not wanting to have sex, and it's not your job to change her mind. All you can do from there is take what she says, respect it, and use the information she gives you to figure out how you can make her more open to the idea of sex.

Talking About Erectile Dysfunction

Erectile dysfunction is not necessarily a common issue in younger men, but with older men it certainly is, and it's something that holds many men back from having sex. But- it shouldn't. It's definitely not as big of an issue as many men assume it will be for their younger woman. And it's totally fine to let your younger lady know that you may have some trouble getting ready for... well, you know.

Believe it or not, most women honestly don't care. Sex for us does not have as big of a stigma attached to it as it does for males. We're totally comfortable just being eaten out, fingered, or aroused in other ways. We do not need penetration to feel as though we've done something really special with someone. So even if it's in the heat of the moment, and you're not prepared or able to have sex, you can still please her- and she will enjoy that, I promise. When you're ready, next time she can please you too.

One big issue many men debate is whether or not to use sex-performance enhancers. In other words- should you or shouldn't you use a pill like Viagra or Cialus? The truth is- it's up to you. What makes you more confident in the bedroom? Do what you want, and I promise your woman will not care. Sex is more emotional, than physical for women- so as long as you're putting in the effort (in whatever technique you choose), she's going to enjoy being in the bedroom with you. And if you do need an extra kick sometimes to get your mind and body in the same place- there is absolutely nothing wrong with popping a pill and letting her experience the rock hard effects.

How To Tell If A Younger Woman Is Using You

Yes, it is 100% true that many younger women use older men. I see this time and time again and each and every time it breaks my heart. Older men become so infatuated with the idea of a younger woman giving them attention that they do not realize they are being walked on, and they end up having their heart broken in the end, wondering what in the world they may have done wrong. They did nothing wrong. They were just blinded by lust- and it's easy to fall into that habit when you're getting the sweet attention of an attractive young female. But there are a few key signs you can definitely look out for that are dead giveaways she isn't truly interested in you for you.

Money is an issue

Most younger women who target older guys in the hopes of using them are after one thing: money. Most of them aren't so serious that they're hoping to get married and collect alimony (although that isn't unheard of). A majority of them simply want to be taken out on a few really expensive nice dates, receive an expensive gift or two, and walk away feeling spoiled and adored. A few key signs that money is an issue can be found on the first date. If she asks how much you make, how much you travel, what kind of car you own, how big your home is, whether or not you pay child support/ alimony (and if so-how much), or blatantly asks for money (even if it's shielded with a sweet story of how she's behind on rent), she may just be after your money. Other signs include hinting at or expecting gifts, never offering to pay for dates, bringing up stories about reasons she may need money- or guilting you into giving her money for things she wants and needs, and being extra sweet to you when you do give her some kind of gift or financial aid- but then being standoffish when the money flow stops.

She's reluctant to introduce you to her friends/ family
Although a large age difference does make introduction to friends and family kind of awkward, if you truly like someone- you're willing to work past those tough moments. If you've been dating for quite some time and she has not offered to introduce you to any of her friends or family members, it may be a sign that she's not totally interested in you. I'd say, once you've reached the 6 month mark of exclusively dating she should have at least introduced you to a few coworkers, friends, or family members. If not, she's either embarrassed or not interested in making things any more serious. At which time you need to evaluate what you actually want out of the relationship and if you're willing to help her work through her issues regarding your age- or simply go along for the ride until it ends.

She's keeping you a secret
She doesn't want to go to places where she may be seen with you by other people she knows. She avoids going on dates with you to places her friends frequent. She won't reply to your phone calls when she's with her friends or family. She avoids your texts at work. In other words, you're a secret- and she only comes to you when she feels like it. Your age difference should not be an excuse for her to feel ashamed of you or to keep you under wraps. Unless you've both consensually agreed to keeping your relationship private for a while, there is zero reason she should not be publicly acknowledging you-

and if she is hiding the fact you're together, her heart isn't in the right place.

She expects odd requests from you (ie nice restaurants, your constant attention)

Younger women would not expect big things out of younger men in a relationship. On the other hand many younger women who use older men, expect older men to go above and beyond in the relationship. They expect constant commitment. They need you to respond to texts, phone calls, and emails immediately. They get upset if you aren't giving them enough attention. They always want to go out to nice restaurants or on expensive dates- and always expect you to pay for them. They expect you to put in ten times more effort than they are, simply because they're younger and they feel you should work for it. The game of cat and mouse, where you're chasing her, can be fun for a while- but eventually it will get exhausting and it will leave you feeling worn out and unappreciated. If a girl is stringing you along in a constant attempt to make you chase her- but not putting in the same amount of effort to chase you in return, it's time to say 'goodbye' and find someone who actually wants to be with you.

She flirts with other men

"Ah- she's just young. She's just having fun," is an excuse I hear from older men ALL the time when we're talking about the fact their younger women is out constantly flirting with other men. But let's face the facts here, if she had eyes only for you- would her eyes be wondering to every other guy in the room? Probably not. So if she ruthlessly flirts with other men in front of you, she's showing you that she's not interested- and most likely she's with you for something other than love.

Becoming Exclusive: Making The Age-Gap Work In A Serious Relationship

The Biggest 'Problem' You'll Face Dating Younger Girls And How To Get Past It

The biggest difference that any May/December relationship needs to overcome is the fact that with your age difference, comes a difference in relationship experience. You've had years of women, you've been through past relationships- you've maybe even been married and divorced and had a family. She on the other hand, does not share those experiences. You may be her first serious relationship. She's probably never been married. She doesn't have decades of dating under her belt. In other words, she's your last love- and you're her first.

I have fallen in love with two older men in my twenty-three years of life. One of which I dated for three years. The other one I dated for a year. My first serious relationship was with a man thirty years my senior, and I fully realize that our differences in relationship experience were our biggest challenge. If you find yourself falling for a woman who's significantly younger than you, and you are her first serious relationship (while she is not yours), then you are inevitably going to run into a few issues. I ran into these same issues, and eventually they would cause my relationship to end. Looking back, the reasons we broke up were entirely preventable, but overcoming the 'biggest problem' does take a lot of effort and willingness to work on things from both ends.

As a young woman, when I originally fell into my three year relationship with a much older man I did not expect to fall as hard as I did. I was in it for fun, and when I found myself actually falling for him, a lot of my own insecurities came bubbling up. He had spent 7 years with another woman and had had two children before I walked into his life. Every woman dreams of marrying a man, and being their first wife. No one imagines walking down the aisle in a white dress to a man who's already been through that experience with another woman. It definitely broke my heart a little bit. I did not like the idea of being a second love, and my boyfriend did not understand my insecurities. Had he really taken the time to understand why I felt the way I did, I think things would have worked out better for us. It's extremely important to take the time with your younger woman and make her feel like she is an entirely separate relationship from your first one. Don't compare her to your ex, don't reference significant moments from your past (like your wedding night or proposal) that will make her feel like she's coming in second place. It's okay to share those things, but don't make them into a huge deal- and don't bring them up often. She doesn't want to hear about your past love anymore than you want to hear about the attractive 24-year-old guy she had sex with before she met you.

It's extremely important that you really set her apart from the last relationship you had. Let her know that she is different, and tell her why she's different. Explain to her that she's made your life better in ways that women in your past have not. Tell her, in detail, why she's different from every other woman you've met in your life. She needs to feel important, and when you've already experienced love with someone else- it's hard for her not to feel second best. Taking the time to let her know that she is a totally different experience than your first love will give her the confidence she needs to push through those insecurities and doubts she may have about you being married or having serious relationships prior to her.

With that being said, the same insecurities can arise in the older guy in the relationship- but in the opposite form. Many older men put a lot of pressure on themselves to be 'the best' their 'last time around' in a relationship. They want to make up for mistakes they've made in the past. They want to make this chance at love worth taking. And that's great, but don't put so much pressure on yourself to be the best for her, that you lose sight of simply having fun and letting love flow the way it naturally does. You don't have to try and make things work. There will be arguments. There will be road blocks. There are in every relationship. What's important is being able to work through those moments and not being hard on yourself when you do make a mistake. It's okay. Remember you're her first love- so she doesn't know what a perfect love is like. All she knows is what you show her. Be the best you can be, and she'll easily be able to overlook the times when you mess up, because she doesn't have anyone else to compare you to. Don't worry so much about being perfect- I promise the fact you're trying to be perfect will make you perfect to her.

Things You Need To Consider Before Getting In A Serious Relationship With A Younger Woman

If you've been dating a younger woman for a while, and you've made things exclusive- before getting too serious, I do think there are a few things you, personally, need to evaluate before continuing the relationship. With an age difference brings a lot of differences in life goals and needs. Being aware of these, and figuring out what sacrifices you're willing to make, will help you prepare for a healthy future with your younger girlfriend.

Kids

Kids are definitely one of the toughest topics for May/December relationships. Most likely you've already had children and she has not. Most women do want kids at some point in time. Not all, but most. Figuring out what her intentions for the future are, and whether or not you share those hopes and dreams, can help prevent heartbreak later on. You should not expect her to not have children, simply to meet your needs. And she shouldn't expect you to have more children if it's not something you're comfortable with. This is a very hard hurdle to overcome, and it does take a lot of introspective thinking on both sides of the relationship. It is by far one of the biggest things I think all younger women and older men need to consider when getting into a serious relationship.

Marriage

Just as with kids, there is a pretty good chance at your older age that you have been married before and she has not. Once again, marriage is a societal norm and it's something many women want to accomplish in their lives. Is getting married a second time something you're comfortable with? Also- is she comfortable with marrying someone who's been married before? This is yet another very important thing to think about. Although neither of you may have the intentions of getting married any time soon, considering the 'what if' of marriage, and whether or not your ideas match up can once again help you have a more meaningful and successful long term relationship.

Career Goals

As you reach retirement, she'll be reaching the height of her working career. Unless you intend to stay in the work field longer while she is also working, there will be a lot of changes that will take place within the household as you each age. Are you willing to go through retirement with a woman who is still active in the workforce? You may have to give up certain investments and traveling plans to meet her work needs. Additionally, she will appear to be the breadwinner in the household during that time frame- as you stay at home, but she is out working. Is this something you're comfortable with. Although this doesn't seem like a huge issue right now, thinking of these things ahead of time, and preparing yourself for the future can help you more readily accept those changes when the time comes.

Life Plans

Everyone has hopes and dreams that they want to accomplish during their life. She may want to travel the world. You may want to take flying lessons. Is traveling a goal you'd like to share this late in your life? Are flying lessons something you will have time for- even if you're having kids and restarting a family with her? Neither of you should have to give up something you truly want to do, to meet the other person's needs because of an age gap. Be aware of the fact you most likely are at different places in your lives and want to accomplish different things with the time you have left. Can you time manage both of your dreams? That's something to consider.

Finances

And lastly, one of the big things to think about are finances. Money. Moo-lah. Yep, we're talking about dollars. Serious relationships, at some point, usually end up combining financial goals and plans (and maybe even bank accounts). Does she spend money the same way do you? Do you have the same financial goals in terms of saving? Does she have any debt (whether it be credit card or school loans) and are you comfortable taking on those kind of financial burdens this late in your life? This may seem like something to discuss before marriage, rather than a serious relationship- but in this modern era combining finances earlier in the relationship is becoming more and more common, and it is something you need to be prepared for.

How To Support Your Younger Woman In Her Career Goals

When you date someone of the same age, you're both typically in the same general place in terms of your career and life goals. On the other hand, when you date someone significantly younger than you, she's most likely at a different spot in her professional life. I feel like older men often want to see their younger girlfriends succeed, but don't quite know how to support them in their career. Contrary to popular belief, younger women don't want you paying off their college loan debt or go out of your way to help them further their career. All they really want is someone who stands beside them and supports them.

Advise without being a know-it-all: I've dated a lot of older men who give me advice with great intentions, but rather than coming off as helpful, they only come off as know-it-alls. They've been in my shoes. They know the ins and outs of the business world, and they want to share their secrets with me. It's awesome, it is. But I just can't help but feel like I'm talking to my father. They'll tell me how to invest my money, or how to approach my boss about a raise or a promotion, or where I should look for work, or how I should move forward in my career. They have a lot of great advice, but rather than motivating me- they usually just come off as pushy and directive. Give her genuine advice that fits the situation. If she feels she isn't getting paid enough at work, explain to her how to go about getting a raise. Don't just pour all of your knowledge on her, because you feel she can benefit. Give her knowledge when the situation arises.

Give her input when she requests, not because you feel you're in a position to: Which brings me to my best point, many older men feel entitled to give advice, because they've been through more in life and they have a more knowledgeable opinion on different subjects. But unwarranted advice isn't always welcome advice. Most likely your younger woman realizes that you have more knowledge than her, and she'll come to you when she wants you to share that knowledge. If you aren't getting the vibe that she's actually looking for advice- don't give it. Wait until she asks first, or is talking to you in a conversation where you can respond with advice without seeming like you're being a know-it-all. It's okay to let her figure a few things out on her own as well. And sometimes, she may want to.

Let her know you believe in her: There is no more amazing feeling in the world, than having your significant other stand behind your dreams. If you're dating a younger woman, 99% of the time she is going to just be starting her dreams- and achieving them is still a ways off. At this point in her life it's so important for her to have a man who stands behind her 100% of the time and lets her know how amazing, talented, and worthwhile she is. Be her biggest supporter and she'll never want to let you go.

Celebrate your achievements, awards, and promotions: I think a lot of older men overlook the smaller achievements more than younger men do- because they've forgotten how much those small achievements mean at a younger age. Her small pay raise, or little promotion, or work award is a HUGE deal to her- especially if it's her first one. Even though this may seem like just another career stepping stone for you, for her this is a big achievement this early in her life. Celebrate with her. She wants someone to be as excited about those things as she is, so don't let your assumptions that they're insignificant get in the way of the fact she is really enthusiastic about them.

Let her shine: At the end of the day, the best couples are the ones who share the spotlight- and know when to let their significant other shine by themselves. Even if you work in the same field (or even the same office), let her have her spotlight sometimes. Let her shine. Let her be the 'big wig', the success story, the one who's career means something. Although you may be at a higher career stature, have a higher pay rate, and generally have more 'work success'- don't let that overshadow her light as well. She deserves to be the special one sometimes in a professional setting, so give her that chance.

Tips For Meeting Your Younger Woman's Parents For The First Time

It's inevitable. At some point, you're probably going to find yourself being introduced to your younger girlfriend's parents. And it will be awkward for everyone involved. You may be the same age as them- you're most likely at least a part of the same generation. You may even be older than them. It's not traditional in any sense, and it can be really uncomfortable, but there are a few ways you can definitely take the pressure off of everyone else.

Begin with just a short introduction (unless they initiate something longer)
Unless they invite you over to a family dinner, or something that involves you being with them for a long period of time- try to plan something relatively short. A quick meet-up at a little cafe, or a nephew's baseball game, or something similar is great. There's no pressure to take anything too seriously when you're only meeting up for a couple moments. You can have a genuine conversation without the pressure to keep a conversation going for hours on end. It gives them a chance to meet you, get a feel for you, process the fact you're dating their much younger daughter, and leaves them time to get used to the idea before getting to know you even better.

Treat them with respect, and as authority figures- even if you're older

In this case, even if they're ten to fifteen years younger than you, they are the adults in the situation. It's their daughter you're with, and naturally they're going to be skeptical of your intentions. Treat them just like you would the parents of someone your own age. Call them "Mr and Mrs." Address them with respect. Let them know you have well-meaning intentions. Answer their questions politely. Show them that you are a gentleman. It may take a while for them to warm up to you, but if you continually prove to them that you are putting in the effort to gain their respect- they will eventually respect you.

Save the touchy feely for another time
It's weird enough for their daughter's boyfriend to be touching her in front of her parents. It's even weirder if that man is the same age as her parents. Just don't do it. It's disrespectful, rude, and will make you appear like a sex-obsessed old man, rather than a respectable boyfriend that they can appreciate their girl being with.

Answer their questions honestly
Chances are, her parents are going to have a few hard questions for you. "Why are you dating my daughter?" "Don't you think your age difference is a bit odd?" and other similar pushy questions could very well be brought up. Be open to them, don't take offense, and answer them honestly and politely. They're curious, and probably a bit worried about your intentions. Put their minds at ease the best you can, by just being truthful with your responses and not taking offense to their seemingly judgmental questions. They have every right to judge, and you're the only one with the power to dismiss their judgments.

How To Properly Introduce Your Younger Girlfriend To Your Kids

For me, as a younger woman, the most nerve-wracking aspect of shackling up with an older man is the idea of meeting their kids. I have been introduced to four different men's children in my twenty-three-years of life and some of those introductions went very well. Others did not go well at all. The truth is, even children as young as six will realize that I'm quite young to be with their dad- and older kids are even more likely to take that realization and look at me with judgment. The hardest scenario, are meeting young adults who are around the same age as me- or even a bit older. Not all men have went about introducing me in the correct way, and looking back I really wish they all would have taken the time to do a few of these things.

Do what's comfortable for you
Of course- first and foremost, do what you're comfortable with as a father. I cannot give you an appropriate time frame to introduce your girlfriend to the kids in. I cannot tell you exactly how to go about the introduction. You know your children better than I could, so use that knowledge and make an intelligent judgment.

Explain to your kids a bit about her ahead of time
I feel one of the biggest mistakes any older man can make when introducing a younger girlfriend to their kids is to simply surprise them. Showing up at an event or meeting with your new girlfriend in tow- having not even said you had a new woman in your life, is extremely rude to your children. How do you expect them to react, when they have not had the chance to process the idea of their dad being with someone else? Before showing them your new woman (no matter how eager you may be to introduce her to them), take a day alone with your kids to talk about her ahead of time. Let them know a bit about who she is, what she likes to do, and why you're dating her (the things you like about her).

Don't make age into a huge deal, but do point it out
Depending on the age of your child, you can approach this subject in different ways- but I believe anyone over the age of ten is entitled to know the age of your girlfriend. Don't make it into a huge deal or the forefront of the conversation, but do let your kids know ahead of time that she is younger than you. Then it won't be such a shock when you introduce her in person and your age difference is evident.

Let them know she makes you happy
The quickest way to gain your children's support in terms of you

dating a younger woman is to let them know that she honestly does make you a happier man. Let your children know that you really do care about her, and you want to have a long relationship with her. Let them see the way she makes you smile and how amazing she makes you feel when she's around. They'll pick up on that happiness, and they'll want their father to be happy.

Avoid drama

This one should seem like an obvious one- but, seriously, all adults in general should just avoid drama in front of kids. When the kids are around they should be the focus of your attention, not some petty argument that you're both continuing from last night. Save that for some other time.

Let her know about your kids likes and dislikes

Prior to introducing your girlfriend to your kids, talk about your kids to her. Let her know what they do in school and for extracurricular activities. Let her know what they like and dislike. She can use this information to talk to the kids, to get to know them, and to share her common interests with them. If she truly cares about you, she's going to put in a lot of effort to get your kids to accept her- and you can give her the tools she needs to do that by letting her know as much about your kids as possible. To the contrast, if she seems disinterested when you're talking about your kids, I strongly believe that she isn't the right woman for you. If a woman loves a man- she loves that man's kids, fair and simple.

Create a fun day activity for the first meeting

You know what your kids enjoy, so make their first time with your new girlfriend enjoyable by taking them somewhere where they'll want to have fun. No kids want to sit across from a fancy dinner table and exchange serious small-talk with adults. Do something fun instead. And yes- this can be done with older kids too. Invite your young adult children to tennis or a museum or even go-cart racing. Do something you know they'll have fun with, and it will take the pressure off of your girlfriend to impress them-because they'll already be impressed with the event.

Figuring Out How To Maintain A Social Life As A Couple

I will openly admit that the biggest struggle I often face when dating older guys is fitting into their social circle- or making them fit into mine. Our age difference makes having a social life pretty tough. We want to bring them along to events with our friends, and they want to do the same for us- but sometimes it just doesn't work out the way we intended it to. Honestly, this is one small hiccup I haven't mastered the art of getting through yet, but I do feel like there are a few things you can keep in mind that will help your social lives stay active without being awkward.

Be aware when your age difference may be inappropriate: For instance, if I'm going to my 5 year high school reunion, chances are my date would definitely be the oldest person there. It'd be like dragging my father along to my homecoming dance. It just won't work. Be aware of the fact that there are just some instances where your age difference won't be appropriate, and rather than making it awkward for everyone else- avoid the situation altogether. It's totally fine to admit that "Hey- we're just not going to look right together at this event" and opt not to go together.

Be honest about your comfort levels: Although her friends may be totally comfortable with you hanging out at their college-frat house party, are YOU comfortable hanging out with a group of people that are all much younger than you? Be truthful about what you are and aren't interested in attending, and expect her to do the same. Once again, it's totally okay to decide that you just don't want to go to a certain event. Your age difference does make a difference in where you feel comfortable, and you both should realize that you both may not always fit in in certain situations.

Do things you both enjoy, with people you're comfortable with: With that being said, you both should put in effort into finding activities that you both can do with friends or family that you both get along with. It's important to have a social life both separately and together as a couple. Being much older, and her being much younger, does make things a bit harder to coordinate. But simple activities like miniature golf, bowling, and eating out are pretty much timeless- and anyone of any age can enjoy them comfortably.

Ease into your relationship with their friends and family (and vice versa): As much as you may want to flaunt your love everywhere you go, realize that the serious age difference is something other people need to get comfortable with in their own time frame. Some people may immediately jump on board and love that you two are in love. Other people may need more time to be okay with the idea. Realize that not everyone will support your decision to be together right away, and give them time to ease into your relationship. Avoid PDA, serious discussions, and overtly romantic gestures early on. Let people get to know you as individuals, and then let them get to know you as a couple. If they like you separately as people, they're going to like you together as a pair. But it's important to give those around you patience as they figure out how they feel about your slightly abnormal pairing.

Important Discussions To Have Prior To 'Popping The Question' To Your Younger Woman

Many men come to me, asking for advice on marrying their younger woman. They feel like they've reached a place in the relationship where they both want to settle down- and they're curious what they can do to make the marriage successful. I believe all marriages should be founded on mutual respect and love. You should both go in realizing that relationships take work and you should be committed to making things continuously better for both of you. With that being said, prior to asking her to marry you- I think there are a few things that are very very important that you discuss together.

Age Difference

Up until this point in the book, I've made it pretty clear that age should not be a huge factor in the relationship. "Age is just a number- it doesn't define who you are" is a motto I live by. But when you are making the promise to stay with someone for the rest of your life, age does become a factor. It becomes a very big factor and it needs to be addressed. You are going to grow older faster than she will. Medical issues may arrive, she may become the caretaker, and there is a very good chance that you will pass away before she does. Talk to her about these things. Although she's probably already aware of this, ask her how she feels. Is she comfortable with the idea of possibly becoming your caretaker? How do you feel about her being your caretaker? How does she feel about the fact that you will not be there with her into her old age? These are definitely things you both need to talk about. It's a tough subject, but it's a healthy one. And by the end of it, both of you should have your minds a bit more at ease about the future- having acknowledged it and knowing one another's comfort zones about it.

Family Health History

Are there any medical histories in your family that may take a toll on your relationship? Do you have many family members who have developed Alzheimer's or dementia? If so- is she prepared for that kind of emotional heartache. You may end up referring to her as your ex, or not even remember her at all. Are there other health conditions prevalent in your family- things like heart problems or skin cancer. What are your chances of developing those same problems, and is she prepared to go through those medical expenses and procedures with you?

Financial Goals

This one's a big one. If you're marrying her- most likely you're planning to combine finances. If not- is she comfortable with that. How do you plan to merge in a financial sense? Will she be a part of your will or life insurance plan? Will you sign a pre-nup? Are you comfortable taking on her student loans, credit card debt, car debt, etc? Where are you both at your financial places in your lives- and can you comfortably combine both of your finances?

Her Wants and Needs

Many older men love the idea of marrying a younger woman and living out their lives traveling in retirement and just being general youthful free-spirits. Most younger women love the idea of that too, but at some point they also want to settle down and have a family. Be aware of her wants and needs and future plans- and how you plan to fit into them. One mistake many older men make when preparing to marry a younger woman is blindly thinking that that woman will give up a lot of her future goals to live out their lives according to your plans. That is an extremely unfair assumption to make, and I definitely think every single older man considering marriage with a younger woman needs to be willing to help her achieve her hopes and dreams as well.

Ending Notes

So, men, to end this guide- what I'd really like to say is just go out there, be confident, be yourself, and find the younger woman of your dreams. There isn't necessarily a magic technique that will get any and every younger woman to swoon at the sight of you, but no matter your financial status, class, appearance, or place in life- as an older guy it is definitely possible for you to meet and keep a younger woman. I've spilled the secrets of a younger woman who has dated older men, and I hope you can use a few of them to your advantage. If you still have additional thoughts, you can absolutely email me at: dawnwhinetaker@mail.com with your questions and comments. I'd be happy to answer them, and maybe even publish an extended version of this book in the future where I address things that I may have missed in these pages.

As for now though, all I truly have to say, is don't be afraid to get out there and try. The one thing that holds many older men back from meeting younger women is that they are just afraid to do so. But that fear is an irrational one. There are definitely younger women out there who are able to fall in love with you- you're goal is to find them and give them the chance to do so. Good luck, and have fun!

17506653R00050

Made in the USA
Middletown, DE
28 November 2018